An Analysis of

Frantz Fanon's

Black Skin,
White Masks

Rachele Dini

Published by Macat International Ltd
24:13 Coda Centre, 189 Munster Road, London SW6 6AW.

Distributed exclusively by Routledge
2 Park Square, Milton Park, Abingdon, Oxon OX14 4RN
711 Third Avenue, New York, NY 10017, USA

Routledge is an imprint of the Taylor & Francis Group, an informa business

www.macat.com
info@macat.com

Cataloguing in Publication Data
A catalogue record for this book is available from the British Library.
Library of Congress Cataloguing-in-Publication Data is available upon request.
Cover illustration: Etienne Gilfillan

ISBN 978-1-912303-73-1 (hardback)
ISBN 978-1-912127-52-8 (paperback)
ISBN 978-1-912282-61-6 (e-book)

Notice
The information in this book is designed to orientate readers of the work under analysis,
to elucidate and contextualise its key ideas and themes, and to aid in the development
of critical thinking skills. It is not meant to be used, nor should it be used, as a
substitute for original thinking or in place of original writing or research. References and
notes are provided for informational purposes and their presence does not constitute
endorsement of the information or opinions therein. This book is presented solely for
educational purposes. It is sold on the understanding that the publisher is not engaged
to provide any scholarly advice. The publisher has made every effort to ensure that
this book is accurate and up-to-date, but makes no warranties or representations with
regard to the completeness or reliability of the information it contains. The information
and the opinions provided herein are not guaranteed or warranted to produce particular
results and may not be suitable for students of every ability. The publisher shall not be
liable for any loss, damage or disruption arising from any errors or omissions, or from
the use of this book, including, but not limited to, special, incidental, consequential or
other damages caused, or alleged to have been caused, directly or indirectly, by the
information contained within.

CONTENTS

THE MACAT LIBRARY

The Macat Library is a series of unique academic explorations of seminal works in the humanities and social sciences – books and papers that have had a significant and widely recognised impact on their disciplines. It has been created to serve as much more than just a summary of what lies between the covers of a great book. It illuminates and explores the influences on, ideas of, and impact of that book. Our goal is to offer a learning resource that encourages critical thinking and fosters a better, deeper understanding of important ideas.

Each publication is divided into three Sections: Influences, Ideas, and Impact. Each Section has four Modules. These explore every important facet of the work, and the responses to it.

This Section-Module structure makes a Macat Library book easy to use, but it has another important feature. Because each Macat book is written to the same format, it is possible (and encouraged!) to cross-reference multiple Macat books along the same lines of inquiry or research. This allows the reader to open up interesting interdisciplinary pathways.

To further aid your reading, lists of glossary terms and people mentioned are included at the end of this book (these are indicated by an asterisk [*] throughout) – as well as a list of works cited.

Macat has worked with the University of Cambridge to identify the elements of critical thinking and understand the ways in which six different skills combine to enable effective thinking.
Three allow us to fully understand a problem; three more give us the tools to solve it. Together, these six skills make up the **PACIER** model of critical thinking. They are:

ANALYSIS – understanding how an argument is built
EVALUATION – exploring the strengths and weaknesses of an argument
INTERPRETATION – understanding issues of meaning

CREATIVE THINKING – coming up with new ideas and fresh connections
PROBLEM-SOLVING – producing strong solutions
REASONING – creating strong arguments

To find out more, visit **WWW.MACAT.COM.**

CRITICAL THINKING AND *BLACK SKIN, WHITE MASKS*

Primary critical thinking skill: ANALYSIS
Secondary critical thinking skill: REASONING

Frantz Fanon's explosive *Black Skin, White Masks* is a merciless exposé of the psychological damage done by colonial rule across the world.

Using Fanon's incisive analytical abilities to expose the consequences of colonialism on the psyches of colonized peoples, the book is both a crucial text in post-colonial theory, and an object lesson in the power of analytical skills to reveal the realities that hide beneath the surface of things.

Fanon was himself part of a colonized nation – Martinique – and grew up with the values and beliefs of French culture imposed upon him, while remaining relegated to an inferior status in society. Qualifying as a psychiatrist in France before working in Algeria (a French colony subject to brutal repression), his own experiences granted him a sharp insight into the psychological problems associated with colonial rule. Like any good analytical thinker, Fanon's particular skill lay in breaking things down and joining dots. His analysis of colonial rule exposed its implicit assumptions and revealed how they were replicated in colonised populations – allowing Fanon to unpick the hidden reasons behind his own conflicted psychological make up, and those of his patients.

Unflinchingly clear-sighted, *Black Skin, White Masks* remains a shocking read today.

ABOUT THE AUTHOR OF THE ORIGINAL WORK

The psychiatrist **Frantz Fanon** was born in 1925 and grew up in Martinique, which was a French colony at the time. His first book, 1952's *Black Skin, White Masks*, was a condemnation of colonial racism that explored the causes and effects of racial prejudice. As Fanon got older, he became increasingly radical, partly because of his involvement in the Algerian War of Independence against France. But he died young, in 1961 aged just 36, from leukaemia. It was mainly after his death that his academic contribution was recognized and appreciated.

ABOUT THE AUTHOR OF THE ANALYSIS

Dr Rachele Dini studied at Cambridge, King's College London and University College London. Much of her current work focuses on the representation of production and consumption in modern and contemporary Anglo-American fiction. She has taught at Cambridge and for the Foundation for International Education, and is now Ledturer in English at the University of Roehampton. Her first monograph, Consumerism, Waste and Re-use in Twentieth-century Fiction: Legacies of the Avant-Garde, was published by Palgrave Macmillan in 2016.

ABOUT MACAT

GREAT WORKS FOR CRITICAL THINKING

Macat is focused on making the ideas of the world's great thinkers accessible and comprehensible to everybody, everywhere, in ways that promote the development of enhanced critical thinking skills.

It works with leading academics from the world's top universities to produce new analyses that focus on the ideas and the impact of the most influential works ever written across a wide variety of academic disciplines. Each of the works that sit at the heart of its growing library is an enduring example of great thinking. But by setting them in context – and looking at the influences that shaped their authors, as well as the responses they provoked – Macat encourages readers to look at these classics and game-changers with fresh eyes. Readers learn to think, engage and challenge their ideas, rather than simply accepting them.

'Macat offers an amazing first-of-its-kind tool for interdisciplinary learning and research. Its focus on works that transformed their disciplines and its rigorous approach, drawing on the world's leading experts and educational institutions, opens up a world-class education to anyone.'

Andreas Schleicher
Director for Education and Skills, Organisation for Economic Co-operation and Development

'Macat is taking on some of the major challenges in university education ... They have drawn together a strong team of active academics who are producing teaching materials that are novel in the breadth of their approach.'

Prof Lord Broers,
former Vice-Chancellor of the University of Cambridge

'The Macat vision is exceptionally exciting. It focuses upon new modes of learning which analyse and explain seminal texts which have profoundly influenced world thinking and so social and economic development. It promotes the kind of critical thinking which is essential for any society and economy.
This is the learning of the future.'

Rt Hon Charles Clarke, former UK Secretary of State for Education

'The Macat analyses provide immediate access to the critical conversation surrounding the books that have shaped their respective discipline, which will make them an invaluable resource to all of those, students and teachers, working in the field.'

Professor William Tronzo, University of California at San Diego

WAYS IN TO THE TEXT

KEY POINTS

- Frantz Fanon (1925–61) was an Afro-French psychiatrist,* philosopher,* and politically radical thinker.

- Published in 1952 and Fanon's first book, *Black Skin, White Masks* addresses the damaging psychological* effects of colonial racism.*

- *Black Skin, White Masks* was a landmark work that anticipated, and helped set the ground for, postcolonial* theory—an inquiry into the legacies of colonial rule.

Who Was Frantz Fanon?

Frantz Fanon, the author of *Black Skin, White Masks* (1952), was an Afro-French psychiatrist and philosopher. Born in 1925 in the French colony of Martinique, he grew up under colonial* rule and as an adult became a passionate critic of the racism that characterized the colonial system. Colonial racism assumed that colonized people were inferior to those of the ruling power, and that their culture and values were also inferior. Based on these assumptions, it imposed its own culture and values on the colonized people, while according them an inferior status within the new society.

Fanon experienced colonial racism from a very young age. In Martinique he became friends with the influential poet, novelist, and political figure Aimé Césaire,* a radical critic of colonialism. Fanon's ideas about racism developed further on serving with the French army during World War II, and when he moved to France to study medicine and psychiatry at the University of Lyon. Qualifying as a psychiatrist in 1951, Fanon intended to submit *Black Skin, White Masks* as his doctoral dissertation. However, the work was considered too controversial and the university examiners rejected it, so Fanon had the manuscript published as a book instead.

In 1953 Fanon was offered a job in Algeria. The Algerian War* for independence from France began the next year. Fanon became involved with the Algerian rebel group *Front de Libération Nationale* (FLN)* in 1955 and as a result, he was expelled from the country in 1957.[1]

His experiences in Algeria had a profound effect on his later writings. In his last book, *The Wretched of the Earth*, Fanon departed from the non-violent tone of *Black Skin, White Masks* and argued that the colonized have the right to commit violence to gain independence. In 1960, Fanon was diagnosed with leukemia; he died the following year, aged just 36.[2] *The Wretched of the Earth* was published after his death.

What Does *Black Skin, White Masks* Say?
In *Black Skin, White Masks* Frantz Fanon argues that colonial racism has psychopathological* effects. In other words, it fosters mentally disturbed behavior. One of his key points refers to the process of cultural assimilation,* a process that occurs when the native culture of a colonized people is replaced by the culture of the colonial power. Fanon argues that this profoundly damages colonized peoples.

This damage, felt on both a collective and on an individual level, occurs in several ways. First, the culture of colonialism prevents the colonized from developing an independent sense of identity, which in turn has a negative effect on their psychological development. Second, because Western popular culture equates whiteness with purity and goodness, and blackness with impurity and evil, the colonized people learn to equate blackness with evil. As a result, they grow up aspiring to be white. This effort to assimilate white culture—and to negate their own black identity—has profound psychological repercussions. It results in a sense of alienation* (that is, doubt as to who they actually are), and with whom they should identify. Sooner or later, Fanon argues, black colonial subjects realize that they have no viable identity. Having learned from an early age that to be black is to be subhuman, they cannot identify as black. At the same time their aspiration to be white is destined to fail, for a black person can never truly become white.

The upshot is that the colonized are caught in an impossible bind. They are both unable to celebrate their native culture, and unable to achieve equality within the colonial culture.

Fanon illustrates this by describing the experiences of different black people encountering their white colonizers for the first time. These stories share a common theme: the shock that black individuals experience upon realizing that, despite their Western European education and loyalty to Western European ideals, white people perceive them to be fundamentally different, and inferior. Colonial culture, Fanon argues, teaches its citizens that the only way to be human is to be white. The colonized internalize this. This deeply embedded message pushes them into an agonizing psychological position. If to be human is to be white, but they are not white, they are forced to see themselves as subhuman.

Fanon's approach was unique for its time. He drew on a range of disciplines to build his arguments. He used Marxism*—an analytical approach to social and economic questions, developed by the German political theorist Karl Marx*—to show that colonial racism is also a socioeconomic issue, and he used the ideas of the influential French psychoanalyst Jacques Lacan* to show that colonialism shapes the world view of its citizens from their earliest years of development.

Fanon also drew from the work of the writers and poets of the Négritude movement,* a literary and philosophical movement developed by African writers resident in France whose work was critical of French colonial rule. In *Black Skin, White Masks*, Fanon shows how the literature of black writers articulates the displaced identity of colonized peoples. He also absorbed the work of existentialist* philosophers such the French intellectual Jean-Paul Sartre.* Existentialism argues that individuals develop by exercising their own free will. Seen in this light, colonialism, which stifles the free will of the colonized, is shown to be inherently dehumanizing.

Finally, Fanon used the experiences of his own psychiatric patients. These revealed the practical, visible effects of colonialism on its citizens.

Why Does *Black Skin, White Masks* Matter?

Frantz Fanon's *Black Skin, White Masks* (1952) was one of the first texts to examine the damaging effects of colonial racism. Fanon's work is also noteworthy for the originality of its approach, which brought together very different schools of thought, including psychology, political theory* and literary criticism.* Fanon turned to the aims and methods of different academic disciplines long before it became commonplace to do so.

Fanon's strident, impassioned tone is also unusual for a work of academic scholarship. *Black Skin, White Masks* is not a dispassionate study of colonial racism. It is a call to arms that urges its black readers to take action against colonialism. While traditional academic writing uses an impersonal tone to maintain scientific objectivity, Fanon does the opposite. By moving between the third, first, and second person— "they," "I," and "you"—he forces the reader to identify with the colonized. His passionate tone suggests that racial oppression must be fought on a personal level. In reading his book we not only gain an insight into the culture of colonialism—we are made to feel its agonizing effects.

For twenty-first century readers, the dehumanizing effects of racism may seem self-evident. Fanon's ideas may not seem worthy of special deliberation but when he was writing, his ideas were highly controversial. They contradicted the popular belief that colonialism was beneficial to the colonized. According to this argument, it was the duty of white people to eradicate the savage impulses of black people and teach them civil behavior. Fanon, instead, asserted that colonialism was destructive, preventing colonized individuals from developing a sense of self. In making these claims, *Black Skin, White Masks* laid the groundwork for new disciplines, including postcolonial and human rights studies.*

Racism is now discussed more openly. In addition, the public perception of racial inequality has shifted significantly since Fanon's day. Nonetheless his text remains relevant to the discussion of race relations. In particular, his ideas help to illuminate the subtle ways in which racism can permeate culture. Despite the advances that have been made, racism still exists. Enduring emblems of racial segregation—such as the Confederate flag in the United States, a flag associated with the desire of the Southern states to preserve the institution of slavery before the American Civil War (1861–65)*—still cause debate. There is still controversy over the insidious role racism plays in news coverage, crime prevention, and government policy. Fanon's ideas are still needed.

NOTES

1   Adam Shatz, "Frantz Fanon: The Doctor Prescribed Violence," *New York Times*, September 2, 2001, accessed August 10, 2015, http://www.nytimes.com/2001/09/02/books/review/02SHATZTW.html

2   Shatz, "Frantz Fanon."

SECTION 1
INFLUENCES

MODULE 1
THE AUTHOR AND THE HISTORICAL CONTEXT

KEY POINTS

- Frantz Fanon's *Black Skin, White Masks* is an important and prescient work of cultural criticism. The book reveals the psychopathological* effects of colonial racism:* in other words, how this form of racism leads to mental disorders and illness.

- Fanon's ideas were shaped by his personal experience of racism while growing up under French colonial rule in Martinique (that is, while Martinique was governed by France).

- Published in 1952, *Black Skin, White Masks* provides a record of the sociopolitical landscape of its time. It gives an insight into the fraught process of decolonization.*

Why Read this Text?

Frantz Fanon's *Black Skin, White Masks* (1952) was one of the first scholarly works to address the effects of colonial racism: discrimination against a colonized people by the ruling power, usually based on the assumption that the ruled are inferior to their rulers. In it, Fanon argues that this form of racism inevitably fosters a sense of dispossession and a crisis of identity in black citizens.

Fanon was a qualified psychiatrist.* Throughout his book he uses examples from his own psychiatric practice to illustrate his argument. But psychiatry is just one of the disciplines he uses to explore his subject. He employs Marxist* philosophy*—the thought and analytical methods of the economist and political theorist* Karl

> ❝ I begin to suffer from not being a white man to the
> degree that the white man imposes discrimination on
> me, makes me a colonized native, robs me of all worth,
> all individuality, tells me that I am a parasite on the
> world, that I must bring myself as quickly as possible
> into the white world ... Then I will quite simply try to
> make myself white: that is, I will compel the white man
> to acknowledge that I am human. ❞
>
> Frantz Fanon, *Black Skin, White Masks*

Marx*—to reveal the socioeconomic dimension of colonial racism.
He draws on the work of Jacques Lacan,* a French psychoanalyst
who had examined the development of identity from early childhood.
By combining this Lacanian psychoanalysis* with the ideas of
phenomenology*—the role that perception plays in the way people
relate to the world—Fanon reveals the very early effects that the
culture of colonialism* has on childhood development, and on
individuals' understanding of the world, and their role within it.

He uses the poetry and prose of writers from the Négritude*
movement (a philosophical and literary movement developed in
France by francophone—French-speaking—African intellectuals and
political figures) to reveal the role that displaced identity plays in the
literature of colonized peoples. Finally, in drawing on the humanist
ideas of the French philosopher Jean-Paul Sartre,* Fanon shows the
dehumanizing effects of colonial culture.

The way in which Fanon combined these different disciplines was
unprecedented, as was the passionate tone of the book. As a result, this
work helped to influence several academic disciplines, including
postcolonial studies* (the study of the various cultural, political, and
psychological legacies of colonialism), sociology* (the study of the
history, structure, and forces that shape society), global diaspora

studies* (the study of the history and consequences of mass migration and the dispersal of people around the globe), and human rights studies.*

Author's Life

Frantz Fanon was born in 1925 in the French colony of Martinique, one of the Caribbean islands. He experienced colonial racism first hand. Growing up in a relatively wealthy middle-class black family, he had a typical French colonial education: classes were taught in French, and students learned to think of themselves as French.[1] However, the contradictions between this and the way his community was treated by the French had a profound effect on Fanon's thought. The community's mistreatment by the pro-Nazi* Vichy* navy—the navy of the government while France was occupied by Germany in World War II* made a particular mark.[2]

Fanon fled from Martinique to serve with the French army in Europe, but returned to Martinique afterward. There, he completed his baccalaureate and campaigned for his friend and mentor, the radical politician and Négritude poet, Aimé Césaire.* But in 1951, Fanon moved from Martinique to France to study medicine and psychiatry. *Black Skin, White Masks* is a modified version of Fanon's doctoral dissertation. Since the examiners rejected the dissertation due to its controversial subject, Fanon published it as a book.

During Fanon's first residency as a psychiatrist he worked for the radical socialist* psychiatrist François Tosquelles.* His second residency was at Blida-Joinville hospital in Algiers, the capital of the North African country of Algeria. In 1954 war broke out between France and Algeria. Fanon sided with the Algerians, and in 1955 he became involved with the *Front de Libération Nationale* (FLN),* the rebel group fighting for Algeria's independence. As a result, he was expelled from Algeria in 1957.

Three years later, while serving as ambassador to Ghana for the provisional Algerian government,* Fanon was diagnosed with leukemia. He died the following year, aged 36. Two of his books were published posthumously in 1961. *Towards an African Revolution* was a series of essays originally written for the Algerian guerrilla information bulletin *El Moudjahid*,* while Fanon's experiences in Algeria shaped the more radical and violent turn of his last work, *The Wretched of the Earth*.

Author's Background

Black Skin, White Masks needs to be understood in the context of the postwar intellectual environment. In the aftermath of World War II, a wave of states gained independence from their European colonial masters. This started with Indian independence in 1947. Being a colonial subject himself, Fanon wanted to show how the racial dichotomy between black and white characterized postwar colonial culture, and how this had a profound psychological effect on the colonized peoples. Fanon's objective was clear: an end to European colonialism. He was also careful to show that colonial racism affected not only black subjects but the white colonizers as well.

Fanon's work reflects his anxiety about the effects of racial hatred on the world. He regularly references *Anti-Semite and Jew* (1946), the seminal postwar study of anti-Semitism*—that is, discrimination against Jewish people—by French existential* philosopher Jean-Paul Sartre,* which showed the cultural roots of ethnic cleansing. Meanwhile, between 1945 and 1949, the Nuremberg trials* (in which the architects of Nazi Germany's program of extermination during World War II were tried for their crimes), exposed the horrors of the Holocaust*—the mass murder of millions of European people, most of whom were Jewish.

Fanon applied Sartre's ideas about the dehumanizing nature of anti-Semitism to that of colonial subjects. Fanon argued, however, that the status of colonized black people was worse than that of Jewish people because of the visibility of their blackness.

NOTES

1   Carol Elizabeth Boyce Davies, *Encyclopedia of the Global Diaspora Experience*, Vol. II (Oxford: ABC-CLIO, 2008), 428.

2   David Macey, "Frantz Fanon, or the Difficulty of Being Martinican," *History Workshop Journal* 58, no. 3 (2004): 211–23.

MODULE 2
ACADEMIC CONTEXT

KEY POINTS

- Because it combines several different disciplines, *Black Skin, White Masks* does not fit easily into any one field.

- Fanon was friends with a number of writers involved in the Négritude* movement and collaborated with the radical politician and writer Aimé Césaire.*

- *Black Skin, White Masks* incorporates ideas from Lacanian psychoanalysis* (that is, the theories of the French psychoanalyst Jacques Lacan,* notably his theories relating to the development of children) and Marxist theory* as well as the views of Fanon's mentor, the psychiatrist* François Tosquelles.*

The Work In Its Context

Frantz Fanon's *Black Skin, White Masks* draws on a number of different disciplines, making it hard to attribute it to one field. One notable influence on Fanon's ideas, however, was the French Négritude movement, to which he makes reference throughout the work. This literary movement emerged in the 1930s when a group of Afro-Caribbean writers in Paris started protesting against French colonial* rule and the imposition of French culture on the colonies: a process known as assimilation.* The most famous writers of the movement were the poet and politician Léon Damas* from French Guiana; Fanon's friend, the Martiniquan poet and politician Aimé Césaire; and the Senegalese poet and politician Léopold Sédar Senghor.*

The movement found inspiration in the artists of the Harlem Renaissance,* which was formed by black artists and writers in New

> ❝ A European familiar with the current trends of Negro poetry ... would be amazed to know that as late as 1940 no Antillean found it possible to think of himself as a Negro. It was only with the appearance of Aimé Césaire that the acceptance of negritude and the statement of its claims began to be perceptible. The most concrete proof this ... is that feeling which pervades each new generation of students arriving in Paris: It takes them several weeks to recognize that contact with Europe compels them to face a number of problems that until their arrival had never touched them. ❞
>
> Frantz Fanon, *Black Skin, White Masks*

York City in the 1920s. The Négritude movement used a variety of inventive ways to expose the alienation* and dispossession that was inherent in colonial life. The Parisian art scene during the interwar years was a very stimulating environment: home to a wide range of radical art movements now known as the avant-garde.* These included cubism* (an approach to pictorial art and sculpture in which the subject is represented from multiple perspectives simultaneously), dada* (a countercultural movement made up of writers, performers, and artists, with a project that mounted a deliberate challenge to rationality in society, politics, and art production) and surrealism* (a movement in the arts influenced by recent discoveries in the field of psychoanalysis, especially the unconscious).

Although the Négritude writers were also experimental, they focused their attention on challenging both colonial rule and the supremacy of white over black culture. Their influence is evident in Fanon's writing style, which often erupts into a kind of prose poetry. The Négritude movement shaped Fanon's belief that to gain independence, the colonized must develop a cultural identity separate to that of their rulers. It also gave him a voice and a style.

Overview of the Field

In *Black Skin, White Masks* Fanon draws on a number of different theoretical frameworks to analyze the colonial experience. These include:

- **Lacanian psychoanalysis**
  This is a form of psychoanalysis that challenges and builds on the ideas of traditional Freudian psychoanalysis. Its founder, Jacques Lacan, was interested in how identity helps to structure human experience. He explored how identity develops, looking at the role of language, culture, social structure, and family. Of these, he considered language to be the most important.

- **Existential humanism***
  Existential humanism is a branch of philosophy.* It views human experience as a process of self-understanding and self-knowledge.

- **Phenomenology***
  Phenomenology is the study of subjective experience. It examines the role that perception plays in the way people relate to the world.

- **Marxist philosophy, or Marxism**
  This is a field of study based on the work of the German political theorist* Karl Marx* (1818–83). It investigates the role of class struggle and social inequality in culture, economics, politics, and history. A Marxist reading of race relations* identifies racism* as a means for whites to exploit black labor, for example by paying blacks less than whites, or not paying them at all. A Marxist reading of colonial relations identifies the resources being exploited by the colonial powers. It recognizes that the system (and its oppressive practices) is driven by the desire for economic gain.

As a trained psychiatrist, Fanon's professional experience also had a profound impact on his writing. His first professional post was under the radical "anti-psychiatrist,"* François Tosquelles. Tosquelles believed that psychiatric treatment could be potentially damaging to patients, arguing that over-medication, electric shock therapy and brain lobotomy were dangerous and dehumanizing. Instead, he advocated using psychiatric techniques to mold patients into "model" citizens. Frequently, this involved ignoring cultural differences in his patients. Fanon's work predated many of the anti-psychiatry movement's most important publications. However, his ideas were shaped by its earliest figures, Tosquelles and Lacan.

Academic Influences

The four people who had the greatest influence on Fanon's work were the French psychoanalyst Jacques Lacan, French philosophers Jean-Paul Sartre* and Marcel Merleau-Ponty,* and the Catalan psychiatrist François Tosquelles.

Fanon makes explicit reference to one of Lacan's key ideas: the mirror stage.* Lacan believed that everyone forms an image of themselves through reference to those around them. Fanon uses this concept to show how black children learn to emulate "white behavior." He also refers to Sartre's articulation of anti-Semitism's* effect on Jewish identity in *Anti-Semite and Jew* (1946), and his description of the French Négritude movement's role in opposing colonial racism in his 1948 essay, *"Orphée Noir."*

Similarly, Fanon's emphasis on the impact of an individual's physical body on the formation of their subjective experience of life can be traced to the teachings of Merleau-Ponty. In his book *Phenomenology of Perception* (1945), Merleau-Ponty related identity to an individual's understanding of themselves as a physical entity.

Fanon's application of these ideas was entirely original, for he also drew attention to the fact that many of those who influenced him were established white scholars with little experience of racism. His work, therefore, went against the grain. Moreover, due to his unorthodox application of these different disciplines, he cannot be said to have been writing in the psychoanalytic, Marxist, or phenomenological tradition. Rather, he combined aspects of each tradition and applied them to race relations under colonial rule, while adhering to a style drawn from the Négritude writers.

MODULE 3
THE PROBLEM

KEY POINTS

- Fanon's work was a response to the racial tensions of his time. He sought to dispel the idea that colonialism* might be of benefit to the colonized.

- Fanon built his argument on the work of several other contemporary radical thinkers.

- *Black Skin, White Masks* seeks to differentiate between simple racial inequality and colonial racism.* Colonial racism treats the colonized as inferior to their colonial rulers on the basis of race. This perception leads those exhibiting colonial racism to expect the colonized to assimilate* the culture of their rulers.

Core Question

Frantz Fanon's *Black Skin, White Masks* was written at a time of immense political upheaval and racial tension. In the early 1950s, colonial communities were seeking independence. Tensions had been mounting in the French colonies since World War I, fueled by the mistreatment of black colonial troops by the French, and by France's failure to recognize the contributions of its colonies to the war effort. In World War II, Fanon experienced this for himself. Following the defeat of the Nazis,* Allied* troops (the military forces of the United Kingdom and the United States, and their allies) crossed the Rhine into Germany. Before photojournalists could document the event, the black soldiers in Fanon's regiment were ordered to go home—a move that ensured they would not feature in the documentation of the French army's victory. These actions fostered tensions with France's colonial subjects, who turned to nationalist sentiment and, eventually,

> ❝ Is there in truth any difference between one racism and another? Do not all of them show the same collapse, the same bankruptcy of man? ❞
>
> Frantz Fanon, *Black Skin, White Masks*

rebellion. Within a few years of World War II, anti-colonial wars broke out between France and its colonies in East Asia and North Africa.

Fanon's text critiques both colonialism and the racial oppression of black people within the colonial system. It therefore takes a stand on the issues of decolonization* (the process by which a nation and its people claim political independence and come to terms with the legacies of colonialism) and racial inequality. The text asks whether France should continue colonial rule, arguing in favor of the right of *all* black people to be independent in thought and identity. To illustrate his point, Fanon explores the dehumanizing effects of colonialism, and reveals the way in which the colonial system destroys its black colonial subjects' sense of identity. In doing so, he upends the imperialist argument that colonialism benefits the colonized and instead demonstrates that it systematically undermines basic human rights. By drawing attention to the violent means used by France to suppress Madagascar's efforts to build its own culture, Fanon debunks the common image of colonial powers as benevolent, caring rulers, and shows instead the lengths to which France would go to maintain control.

The Participants

Fanon's text contains arguments in favor of racial equality and decolonization. In the United States, important postwar figures in the discussion about race relations included the African American political activist Martin Luther King* and the African American human rights activist Malcolm X.* In France they included the French philosopher

Jean-Paul Sartre* and the Négritude* poet Aimé Césaire.* The poets and writers of the Harlem Renaissance* (a black literary movement that began in the New York City of the 1920s) were also involved, along with the French Négritude movement. All of these people argued against the racist treatment of black people and championed the acceptance of black human rights.

The debate around decolonization was wider and more complex than the debate around racial equality, in part because it involved debunking the argument that colonialism was beneficial to the colonized, and demonstrating that colonialism was exploitative in nature. For anti-colonialists, colonialism's policy of cultural assimilation*—encouraging the colonized community to take on the culture of the colonial power—was just a further form of racism. Both were tools that enabled the governing country to make use of its colonies' natural resources and labor force. Fostering loyalty to the colonial power's culture and a sense of inferiority in the colonized people helped to ensure that they would not seek better living conditions. The system relied on the governed identifying with, and feeling inferior to, the colonial power.

A key figure who spoke out about this was Ghana's first president, Kwame Nkrumah,* an influential player in the French colonies' battle for independence. Important contributions also came from figures less closely involved in the struggle. For example, in 1952, the French demographer Alfred Sauvy* coined the term "Third World"* to define developing countries hitherto exploited by global powers. By articulating the impoverished state of developing countries, Sauvy's work marked an important moment in postwar discussions about the distribution and concentration of global power.

The Contemporary Debate

The full import and originality of Fanon's views cannot be fully understood without looking at the writing of the scholars who influenced his thinking. What is impressive about his work is that he engages with the contentious topic of colonial racism through such a diverse and disparate range of academic disciplines. This approach allows him to examine aspects of the issue in a way that had hitherto been ignored.

The most noteworthy of Fanon's theoretical applications is his use of Sartre's writings on anti-Semitism* and the French Négritude movement. In his 1946 work *Anti-Semite and Jew,* Sartre examined the "rationale" of anti-Semitism and the effect it had on Jewish identity. While the book specifically addressed racism against the Jewish people, it tapped into the cultural mood of the time, relating to broader anxieties about the impact of racism. Fanon uses Sartre's ideas to link the condition of colonized peoples with the recent horrors of the Holocaust* (the mass murder sponsored by Nazi Germany during World War II, in the course of which many millions were killed—some six million of whom were Jewish).

Fanon was also influenced by Sartre's *"Orphée Noir."* This was an essay about the French Négritude movement,* which Sartre wrote as an introduction to a collection of poetry edited by the Senegalese Négritude poet Léopold Sédar Senghor.* Sartre's essay helped introduce the movement to (white) French intellectuals. Using Hegelian dialectic* (an approach to resolving problems in which an argument is met with a counterargument, before a conclusion is reached that reconciles the two sides), Sartre argued that Négritude embodied an ideology that was the exact opposite of colonial racism—"anti-racist" racism. Fanon builds on Sartre's ideas, but he also critiques them, arguing that Sartre's understanding of alienation* in his other work, *Being and Nothingness*, falls short when applied to black people.[1] In particular, he notes that black people living under Western rule experience alienation of a different, and fundamentally more brutal, kind: the society into which they are born is inherently alienating, for it sees blackness itself as foreign, and "wrong."

NOTES

1   Frantz Fanon, *Black Skin, White Masks* (London: Pluto Press, 1986), 106.

MODULE 4
THE AUTHOR'S CONTRIBUTION

KEY POINTS

- Frantz Fanon's *Black Skin, White Masks* investigates the psychopathological* effects of colonial racism*—that is, the manifestations of psychological distress that it causes.

- Although *Black Skin, White Masks* remained largely obscure in the two decades following its publication, the work found a new audience in the late 1970s and early 1980s. It gained popularity following the emergence of postcolonial studies* (the academic inquiry into the various legacies of colonialism).*

- *Black Skin, White Masks* stands out for its highly original application of a number of different disciplines.

Author's Aims

Frantz Fanon's *Black Skin, White Masks* is both a significant work of scholarship and a powerful condemnation of the structure of colonialism* itself. Fanon's aim was to illustrate the insidious role that colonial racism plays in fostering feelings of dispossession and alienation* in the colonized. He argues that it teaches the colonized that they are subhuman. It presents them with an impossible task: of relinquishing their "blackness," and of aspiring, from infancy, to be— and to be thought of—as white. Colonial racism teaches the colonized that only whites are human. So the colonized continuously aspire to be something they cannot be, and their inability to be white becomes the confirmation of their subhuman status.

This impossible situation breeds mental disorder; colonial racism forces the subject to forge a new identity, but also reminds them, at every turn, that the identity they have appropriated is illegitimate.

> 66 [There] is a constellation of postulates, a series of propositions that slowly and subtly—with the help of books, newspapers, schools and their texts, advertisements, films, radio—work their way into one's mind and shape one's view of the world of the group to which one belongs. In the Antilles that view of the world is white because no black voice exists. 99
>
> Frantz Fanon, *Black Skin, White Masks*

As well as showing how this psychopathology develops, Fanon argues that it can endure even after decolonization* (the process by which a nation rids itself of colonial government and the cultural and political legacies of colonialism). Given that colonialism imposes the culture of the colonial power on its colonies, newly decolonized nations run the risk of finding themselves in a cultural vacuum. To prevent this from happening, he argues that postcolonial nations must take steps to develop an independent culture and identity.

Approach

Fanon was not alone in his anti-colonialist stance. Nor was he alone in identifying the inherent racism in colonialism's policy of cultural assimilation. His approach to these issues, however, was highly original. In combining ideas from a number of different fields and using both psychiatric* cases and literary extracts to build his argument, Fanon developed a unique work of scholarship.

One of Fanon's key inspirations was the work of the French philosopher Jean-Paul Sartre.* Like Fanon, Sartre combined existential humanism* (a philosophy that emphasizes the idea that human experience is a process of self-understanding and self-knowledge) with the economic and social philosophy* and analysis of Marxism* in his critiques of racial and social inequality. Sartre also wrote at length about French Négritude* in his essay of 1948, *"Orphée*

Noir." While Fanon engages with Sartre's ideas, he moves beyond them to develop his own understanding of colonial racism. He is careful, as well, to call for action; his suggestion that action may result in the world he desires makes Fanon's vision of the future less bleak than that of Sartre.

Fanon's work is distinguished by its intensely passionate tone and literary style. His use of literary devices such as stream-of-conscious narration* and multiple narrative perspectives* makes *Black Skin, White Masks* a compelling work of literature as well as scholarship. The palpable anger throughout the text is a reminder of Fanon's political intent: this is a work of scholarship, but it is also a call to action.

Contribution in Context

Fanon's work stands out for his interdisciplinary approach and his vivid writing style. It is also noteworthy for the way in which it acknowledges the limits of theory in tackling oppression. Fanon is aware that fighting oppression is, ultimately, a practical issue.

These attributes distinguish Fanon's work from the anti-colonialist writings of his contemporaries. They also distinguish it from the theorists who inspired him, such as the Catalan psychiatrist François Tosquelles.* It was while working for Tosquelles that he learned how culture can affect psychology. He was also inspired by the French psychoanalyst Jacques Lacan* and by the process Lacan describes, in which young children are drawn to identify with those around them. But Fanon was the first to apply the ideas of these theorists to understanding colonial racism and how the process of assimilation* affects development—noting, for instance, that black children under colonialism learn to identify as white.

Similarly, although Fanon's ideas about the cultural aspects of racism were shaped by Sartre's study of anti-Semitism,* Fanon built his argument very differently. He also used a very different theoretical framework. Although he drew heavily on the ideas of the French

Négritude movement—going as far as to emulate the writing style of the Martiniquan poet Aimé Césaire*—his adoption of these ideas was highly original. His writing style combined political manifesto with stream-of-conscious narrative and academic study. It was a new kind of essay form, made to fit Fanon's revolutionary purposes.

SECTION 2
IDEAS

MAIN IDEAS

KEY POINTS

- *Black Skin, White Masks* is concerned with racial oppression, cultural assimilation,* and dehumanization* under colonialism.*

- Fanon argues that colonial racism* fosters psychopathological* tendencies in both the oppressors and the oppressed—that is, the undesirable manifestations of psychological* distress.

- Fanon structures his argument around four main points, which he reiterates throughout the seven essays in his book.

Key Themes

There are two core themes in Frantz Fanon's *Black Skin, White Masks*: dehumanization and the psychopathology of colonial racism.

Describing dehumanization, Fanon shows how the system of colonialism strips its citizens of their human status; treats them as inferior to whites; teaches them that the only way to be considered human is to act white; and teaches them to identify with the culture of their oppressors.

Discussing the psychopathology of colonial racism and assimilationism, Fanon argues that the dehumanizing effects of colonial racism, in turn, foster psychopathological tendencies. Colonialism forces the oppressed into a double bind. On the one hand, they are told that the only way they will be considered human is if they act white. On the other hand, their encounters with white people remind them that they *are not* white, and can never *be* white. Black

> ❝ In this work I have made it a point to convey the misery of the black man. Physically and affectively. I have not wished to be objective. Besides, that would be dishonest: It is not possible for me to be objective. ❞
> Frantz Fanon, *Black Skin, White Masks*

people under colonialism therefore live with the belief that they are inferior, and that nothing they do will rectify that condition.

Fanon explores the effects of colonial racism on four areas of life: childhood development; the treatment of black colonials upon their arrival in France; sexual relations between blacks and whites; and the cultural myths and assumptions associated with the concept of "blackness." In each instance, Fanon shows how colonialism unleashes deep-seated prejudices, ensuring that whites feel disgust for blacks, and that blacks feel inferior to whites.

These feelings of self-loathing and inferiority are difficult—if not impossible—for colonized peoples to eradicate. Even if the colonies succeed in overthrowing their rulers, they will face the difficult task of reconstructing their communities. This idea of reconstruction is crucial. For Fanon, it is imperative that the colonies develop an independent identity to replace the French culture imposed on them during colonialism. To be truly autonomous* (that is, independent), they must replace French with their native language, develop a national identity of their own, and take pride in that identity.

Exploring the Ideas

In exploring colonial racism, Fanon is looking to the future. His aim is to help the colonies flourish once they have gained independence.

First, he notes that colonialism interferes with the formation of personal identity. All human beings develop in relation to their cultural environment. Popular myths are ingrained in the stories they hear as children and in the media and Western (colonial) popular culture equates blackness with evil. The stories and nursery rhymes that teach small children the difference between good and bad also teach them that to "be good" is to "be white." So black children under colonialism are taught to renounce their racial identity.

Fanon's second argument is that black identity under colonialism does not develop in its own right. It always exists in relation to the culture of the white colonial rulers. His title *Black Skin, White Masks* refers to this assimilation: "It is not I who make a meaning for myself, but it is the meaning that was already there, pre-existing, waiting for me."[1] Black people under colonialism are forced to adapt to a pre-existing set of criteria. They are forced to wear a "white mask."

Third, Fanon argues that colonialism creates the ideal conditions for psychopathological behavior. To force the colonized to "act white" forces them to disown their native culture. Moreover, this masquerade *cannot work*. At some point the colonized individual will be faced with the fact that she or he is *not* white, can never *be* white, and that for white people, she or he is the evil "other." This is traumatic: in learning how white people perceive them, the colonized recognize their subhuman status. Fanon viewed this dilemma as a central cause of the mental disorders of his psychiatric* patients. He argued that to truly emancipate* themselves—make themselves entirely free—the colonies would need to develop their own cultural identity and eradicate French influences.

These ideas may seem self-evident today but when Fanon was writing, they were highly controversial. They contradicted the commonly held belief that colonialism enabled colonized people to join civilization.

Language and Expression

Black Skin, White Masks is as unique for its writing style as it is for its argument. Fanon's tone is impassioned, and often angry. The text itself moves frequently between the first,* second* and third person,* often within the space of a paragraph. At times, the paragraphs themselves give way to fragmented, disjointed sentences resembling prose poetry more than reasoned argument. Fanon does this intentionally: the shift between "I" and "you," "they" and "we," disorientates the reader. The feeling of ambiguity and confusion created by this helps convey the sense of alienation* felt by the colonized. The use of stream-of-conscious narration*—roughly, a device frequently used by early twentieth-century novelists and poets to convey alienation, shock, or mental disorder, in which thoughts are related in an unmediated stream—helps underpin the psychopathological effects of colonial racism.

The text's other distinguishing feature is its use of literary texts and examples from Fanon's own psychiatric practice. This is highly unusual for a psychiatric or sociological* study. By using the literature produced under colonial rule to study the effects of racism, Fanon gives voice to the dispossessed. Moreover, he relates extracts of poetry by writers of the Harlem Renaissance* and French Négritude* to the experiences of his own psychiatric patients. In doing so, he intensifies the effect of both. The examples from his practice highlight the reality of the experiences depicted in the poetry, while the poetic style of the extracts renders the examples themselves more vivid.

NOTES

1   Frantz Fanon, *Black Skin, White Masks* (London: Pluto Press, 1986), 102.

SECONDARY IDEAS

KEY POINTS

- Frantz Fanon's investigation of both interracial relations and cultural assumptions about black genitalia remains an underexplored area.

- Fanon's deductions on these themes are interesting, but not as central to his core argument as his theories about language and cultural assimilation.*

- For this reason, and because some of his assumptions about sexuality are dated, the ideas expressed in these two chapters have received less attention.

Other Ideas

The main secondary theme of Frantz Fanon's *Black Skin, White Masks* is his discussion of interracial relationships. He devotes two chapters of his text to this issue, entitled, "The Woman of Color and the White Man," and "The Man of Color and the White Woman."

Fanon argues that interracial relationships are governed by the desire to "whiten" the black race by diluting the bloodline. He claims that the black woman's desire to "better" herself and the black man's desire to "reclaim his dignity" prompt them to seek white partners. The desire is therefore rooted in self-hatred. It stems from the perception that one's own race is flawed or viewed as an obstacle to overcome. In this sense, interracial mixing is psychologically* problematic. However, Fanon emphasizes that the problems he perceives in interracial mixing are caused by racism. He is not promoting segregation: he is explaining that the damaging effects of

> 66 As for the Negroes, they have tremendous sexual powers. What do you expect, with all the freedom they have in their jungles! They copulate at all times and in all places. They are really genital. They have so many children that they cannot even count them. Be careful, or they will flood us with little mulattoes. 99
>
> Frantz Fanon, *Black Skin, White Masks*

colonial racism* extend to sexual relations. Under colonialism,* black people are viewed as inferior; this shapes the way in which both genders are perceived sexually.

Fanon extends these ideas in another chapter, "The Negro and Psychopathology."* Here, he examines cultural myths about the size of black men's genitalia to explore how this shapes the attitudes of white men and women toward black men. He argues that the perception that black men have larger genitals plays a role in their subjugation,* because white men are jealous of black men on a "genital level."[1] In this context, racial oppression is merely a paranoid reaction to the white man's anxieties that black men will steal their women.[2] When a white man sees a black man, he "is no longer aware of the Negro but only of a penis; the Negro is eclipsed. He is turned into a penis. He *is* a penis."[3] Reducing the black man to a set of genitals reaffirms his uncivilized, subhuman status and justifies the oppressor's fears. Therefore, the body itself becomes a tool for racial oppression.

Exploring the Ideas

In "The Woman of Color and the White Man," Fanon explores relations between black women and white men under colonialism by looking at the autobiographical work of the French Martiniquan writer Mayotte Capécia.* He uses her hugely successful memoir of 1948, *Je suis Martiniquaise*, to explore the tension between the black colonial woman's aspiration to marry a white man, and her recognition that she will never be seen as "altogether respectable in a white man's eyes."[4]

Fanon views the memoir's popularity among black Martiniquan women as a reflection of their self-identification with Capécia's plight. Black women under colonialism aspire to find a white man, and that aspiration is part of a broader aspiration to "magically [become] white."[5] Fanon argues that this aspiration is rooted in the socioeconomic conditions of black colonials. As Fanon puts it, "historically, inferiority has been felt economically," and "one is white above a certain financial level."[6] Marriage to a white man promises both emancipation* from the social inferiority suffered by black colonials, and from economic duress. On a more subconscious level, Fanon says, the black woman looks to reproduce with the white man in order to "whiten the race."[7]

Fanon goes on to show that even black sexual relations are governed by the desire to "whiten the race": "every woman in the Antilles, whether in a casual flirtation or in a serious affair, is determined to select the least black of men."[8] In each case, the relationship is shaped, at heart, by the black woman's desire to "save the race."[9] This aspiration forms part of the psychopathology* of colonial racism because at its core lies the assumption that white is superior to black.

In "The Man of Color and the White Woman," Fanon argues that relations between the black colonial man and the white woman are governed by the black man's desire to "grasp white civilization and dignity and make them [his]."[10] In other words, sleeping with a white woman is an act of self-assertion, and of dominance.

Overlooked

Fanon's discussion of the role played by colonial racism in sexual relations is important. So too is the way he identifies the numerous preconceptions held by the West about the black male body and about black sexuality. His analysis draws attention to a number of flawed assumptions and shows the insidious role these have played in colonial oppression. In the early nineteenth century, for example, white colonial rulers were known to cut off and display black male genitalia.[11] This illustrates the highly politicized nature of sexual relations between the races.

There are two main reasons why Fanon's ideas about interracial sexual relations remain underexplored by scholars. The first is that the study of sexuality and the discipline of body politics are both relatively recent, and have lagged behind the civil rights movement* and decolonization* by some 20 years. Fanon's ideas are frequently used in postcolonial studies,* which emerged in the late 1970s and early 1980s. In contrast, the study of sexual politics and race only gained traction in the early to mid 1990s. Second, Fanon's ideas about sexuality are limited by the fact that he only considers heterosexual* relationships and does not assume equality between the sexes. In the examples he uses, the women of both races play a passive role. Women are essentially transacted between black and white men. So discussions about gender in Fanon's thought tend to focus on his treatment of women, and ask whether his depiction of them as passive is a sign of contempt that detracts from his message, or if he is addressing race at the expense of women, but without malicious intent.[12]

NOTES

1   Frantz Fanon, *Black Skin, White Masks*, (London: Pluto Press, 1986), 121.

2   Fanon, *Black Skin, White Masks*, 123.

3   Fanon, *Black Skin, White Masks*, 130.

4   Mayotte Capécia, *Je suis Martiniquaise* (Paris: Corréa, 1948), 202.

5   Fanon, *Black Skin, White Masks*, 32.

6   Fanon, *Black Skin, White Masks*, 32.

7   Fanon, *Black Skin, White Masks*, 33.

8   Fanon, *Black Skin, White Masks*, 33.

9   Fanon, *Black Skin, White Masks*, 38.

10 Fanon, *Black Skin, White Masks*, 45.

11 David M. Friedman. *A Mind of its Own: A Cultural History of the Penis* (New York: Simon and Schuster, 2001), 143.

12 T. Deanean Sharpley-Whiting. *Frantz Fanon: Conflicts and Feminisms* (Oxford: Rowman & Littlefield, 1998), 47.

MODULE 7
ACHIEVEMENT

KEY POINTS

- Frantz Fanon's *Black Skin, White Masks* is exceptional in the way it articulates the inherently dehumanizing* tendencies of the colonial* system.

- The work stands out for its eloquence, its sophisticated scholarship and its anticipation of ideas that other scholars would not develop for another two decades.

- Because the work was ahead of its time, it was largely overlooked for many years, only gaining a following after Fanon's death in 1961.

Assessing The Argument

Frantz Fanon's first work, *Black Skin, White Masks* reveals the dehumanizing effects of colonial racism.* Fanon argues that forcing the colonized to assimilate the culture of their rulers, while at the same time reminding them that they are outsiders, results in alienation* at best. At worst, it results in destructive psychosocial behavior.

Both Fanon's argument and the way he developed it were highly original. His interdisciplinary* approach (that is, an approach drawing on the aims and methods of different academic disciplines) was ahead of its time. It allowed Fanon to address colonial racism from a multitude of angles, revealing its effect on childhood development; individual identity; social relations; socioeconomic inequality; and class tension. This resulted in a much more complex argument than simply stating that colonialism is unfair, and that treating blacks differently from whites is wrong.

> " All forms of exploitation are identical because all of
> them are applied against the same 'object': man. When
> one tries to examine the structure of this or that form
> of exploitation from an abstract point of view, one
> simply turns one's back on the major, basic problem,
> which is that of restoring man to his proper place.
> Colonial racism is no different from any other racism.
> Anti-Semitism hits me head-on: I am enraged, I am
> bled white by an appalling battle, I am deprived of the
> possibility of being a man. "
>
> Frantz Fanon, *Black Skin, White Masks*

What Fanon revealed were a number of fundamental flaws in the very system of colonialism. These flaws rendered the system indefensible. Fanon showed that colonialism teaches the colonized that they are subhuman, and encourages them to "act white." When these efforts inevitably fail, the colonized internalize that failure, and view it as a reflection of their own shortcomings. In short, colonialism is primed to breed mental disorder.

Achievement in Context

Black Skin, White Masks was masterful both in its scholarship and in its literary eloquence. It was also ahead of its time. When it was published in 1952, racial tensions between France and its colonies were high, but it was only after France's devastating defeat in the Algerian War* in 1962 that the discussion of colonialism became mainstream. And it was not until the mid-1980s that academic scholarship addressed the enduring legacy of colonialism on culture as a whole. For these reasons, Fanon's text was largely overlooked in academic circles for several decades. It was only as events unfolded in Algeria and anti-colonialist sentiment gained momentum in academic circles that it ignited renewed interest. The legacy of the book has been an enduring one. It served as the intellectual basis for the emergence of postcolonial studies* in the 1980s and a key source for diaspora studies* (that is, the study of the consequences and legacies of a community or people's international dispersal) and human rights studies* in the late 1990s and early 2000s, all of which served to cement its canonical status.

Published in 1961, a year before the end of the Algerian War, *The Wretched of the Earth* met with a far warmer reception than *Black Skin, White Masks*. Media coverage of the Algerian War had raised public awareness of the French colonies' plight both in France and in other countries. 1961 in particular saw several acts of violence in metropolitan France that made the public far more aware of the plight of the Algerians. One of these incidents was the Paris Massacre* of 1961, in which French police ambushed a forbidden demonstration of 30,000 Algerians in support of the FLN* (the National Liberation Front). The numbers killed are still debated. These events paved the way for Fanon's final book, creating a much more receptive audience for his ideas.

Limitations

Black Skin, White Masks is an undeniably sophisticated work of scholarship and remarkably prescient in its understanding of racial tensions. Nonetheless certain aspects of the text are problematic. Contemporary scholars have pointed out that the work reflects antiquated—and somewhat misogynistic* (that is, founded on an offensively sexist perspective)—views of women and of female sexuality.[1] For Fanon, women are objects for which black and white men compete to assert their status.[2] In this sense, Fanon's call for equality between the races is actually a call for equality between men alone.

Fanon confines his ideas about sexual relationships between the races to heterosexual ones and expresses homophobic* views in several instances.[3]

The Canadian academic Terry Goldie has criticized Fanon's categorization of homosexuality as a psychopathological* disorder, for example. Fanon says the desire of black women to sleep with or marry white men is a form of racist self-loathing, or "negrophobia." He asserts: "the Negrophobic woman is in fact nothing but a putative sexual partner—just as the Negrophobic man is a repressed homosexual."[4] Goldie notes that for Fanon, homosexuality is one way in which hatred of one's race is expressed, making it a symptom of colonialism. It is, in other words, a means whereby black men under colonialism are objectified*—made passive by being turned into "objects."[5] According to Fanon's logic, homosexuality among blacks would cease to exist were colonialism to end.

The British sociologist* Jonathan Dollimore uses Fanon's reading of homosexuality as a case study in what he calls "sexual dissidence"— sexuality and sexual relations that differ from, or actively oppose, mainstream sexual behavior.[6] Dollimore says that in some black communities, homosexuality is viewed as "the white man's disease."[7] He also discusses the important role played by masculinity in cultures of resistance. In this context "masculinity [is] inseparable from [the] fight for liberation."[8] While the effect of such a "macho" attitude is to "[perpetuate], in terms of sexual and gender relations, the very oppression being resisted at other levels," Dollimore argues that Fanon's articulation of it is profoundly revealing; it provides a better understanding of the powerful role of sexuality in racial oppression.[9]

NOTES

1   See Madhu Dubey. "The 'True Lie' of the Nation: Fanon and Feminism," *Differences: A Journal of Feminist Cultural Studies* 10, no. 2 (1998): 1–29; and Tracy Denean Sharpley-Whiting, *Frantz Fanon: Conflicts and Feminisms* (Lanham, Maryland: Rowman & Littlefield, 1998).

2   Linda Lane and Hauwa Mahdi, "Fanon Revisited: Race Gender and Coloniality Vis-à-vis Skin Colour," *The Melanin Millennium: Skin Color as 21st Century International Discourse*, Ronald E. Hall, ed. (Dordrecht: Springer Science + Business Media, 2013), 169–81.

3   See Terry Goldie, "Saint Fanon and Homosexual Territory," *Frantz Fanon: Critical Perspectives* (1999), 77–88; and Karen Lovaas, *LGBT Studies and Queer Theory: New Conflicts* (London: Routledge, 2013), 216–20.

4   Fanon, *Black Skin, White Masks* (London: Pluto Press, 1986), 121.

5   Goldie, "Saint Fanon," 79, 83.

6   Jonathan Dollimore, *Sexual Dissidence: Augustine to Wilde, Freud to Foucault* (Oxford: Oxford Paperbacks, 1991), 345.

7   Dollimore, *Sexual Dissidence*, 345.

8   Dollimore, *Sexual Dissidence*, 347.

9   Dollimore, *Sexual Dissidence*, 347.

MODULE 8
PLACE IN THE AUTHOR'S LIFE AND WORK

KEY POINTS

- *Black Skin, White Masks* was Fanon's first book. It articulated ideas that he spent the next eight years developing.

- The text is distinctly different in both tone and argument from Fanon's later writing.

- Although *Black Skin, White Masks* marks an important chapter in Fanon's intellectual career, and in the history of decolonization,* it is a good idea to read it alongside his other work.

Positioning

Black Skin, White Masks was the first of Frantz Fanon's published works and was written when he was a doctoral student. The text can be seen as containing—in embryonic form—some of the key ideas that would preoccupy him for the next decade. These include the concern with racial equality, and the link between oppressive regimes and psychopathological* behavior, which are at the heart of all his work.

However, *Black Skin, White Masks* differs in several important ways from Fanon's later writings. Like them, it is impassioned, angry, and vocally anti-colonialist.* However, it is more concerned with understanding the root causes of black people's alienation* under colonial rule, and championing the search for a new identity, than it is with inciting violence. It is much more theoretical, and grounded in philosophical* ideas, than his later writings. The urgent tone of his later work is overtly aimed at changing the status quo, rather than with understanding its origins

> **❝** I meet a Russian or a German who speaks French badly. With gestures I try to give him the information that he requests, but at the same time I can hardly forget that he has a language of his own, a country, and that perhaps he is a lawyer or an engineer there. In any case, he is foreign to my group, and his standards must be different. When it comes to the case of the Negro, nothing of the kind. He has no culture, no civilization, no 'long historical past. **❞**
>
> Frantz Fanon, *Black Skin, White Masks*

After writing *Black Skin, White Masks*, Fanon's aspirations changed. Whereas he wrote this first book from the perspective of a black man who saw himself as French, and was looking to gain legitimacy among white people in France, his later writings break definitively with European culture. In the decade following the publication of *Black Skin, White Masks*, he embraced the task of inciting colonized peoples to take back their lands and their dignity. These later texts are far more concerned with the fate of *all* black people in a way that *Black Skin, White Masks* was not.

Integration

Fanon's later writings grew more violent as he became more involved in the anti-colonialist movement. His last book was *The Wretched of the Earth* (1961), which was published after his death. In this, he argues that because colonial power relies on military strength, the only way to overthrow it is with violence. For Fanon, the colonists impose violent resistance on the colonized. This work is much less theoretical than *Black Skin, White Masks*. It focuses on the obstacles that newly free people will face in the process of decolonization. *The Wretched of* *the Earth* is the product of Fanon's first-hand experiences of the Algerian War.*

If *Black Skin, White Masks* does not deal as explicitly or exhaustively with violence as Fanon's later writings, it does however presage some of his later ideas. For example, it already shows a concern with the aftermath of decolonization. "In no way should I derive my basic purpose from the past of the peoples of color. In no way should I dedicate myself to the revival of an unjustly unrecognized Negro civilization. I will not make myself the man of any past. I do not want to exalt the past at the expense of my present and of my future."[1] This is a key passage. It reveals Fanon's preoccupation with shaping the future and shows that, even in the initial stages of his career, his philosophy was one of action.

Comparing *Black Skin, White Masks* with Fanon's later writings reveals the evolution of his intellectual thought. The book stands out in its effort to reconcile thought and action; ultimately, however, Fanon points to the limits of theoretical studies in combatting oppression and argues passionately for the need for action.

Significance

Black Skin, White Masks only gained influence several decades after Fanon's death. Its revival was due to the emergence of postcolonial studies* as a field of study.* As scholars began to consider the enduring legacy of colonialism*—including its role in our understanding of particular historical events, literary artifacts, and cultural myths—Fanon's work took on new meaning. In this sense, his writing was very much before its time.

Within Fanon's own body of work, *Black Skin, White Masks* is generally less acclaimed than his last book, *The Wretched of the Earth* (1961). However, this has less to do with the works themselves than with when they were published, and the world into which they were born. *The Wretched of the Earth* was published in 1961, at the tail end of the Algerian War. This was also six or seven years into the American Civil Rights Movement:* the movement to secure equal rights for black people in the United States. *The Wretched of the Earth* therefore had a much more receptive audience than *Black Skin, White Masks* and it was immediately heralded as a revolutionary work. Moreover, the French philosopher Jean-Paul Sartre* provided its preface, which cemented the text as the work of a great intellectual. Sartre wrote that the "Third World finds *itself* and speaks to *itself* through [Fanon's] voice."[2]

NOTES

1   Frantz Fanon, *Black Skin, White Masks* (London: Pluto Press, 1986), 176.

2   Jean-Paul Sartre, preface to *The Wretched of the Earth*, trans. Constance Farrington (London: Penguin, 2001), 9.

SECTION 3
IMPACT

MODULE 9
THE FIRST RESPONSES

KEY POINTS

- Frantz Fanon originally submitted *Black Skin, White Masks* as a doctoral thesis but the board of examiners rejected it because its subject matter was seen as too controversial.

- Because decolonization* was such a fraught topic, the initial reception to Fanon's work was very limited. The book remained relatively obscure for over a decade after his death.

- *Black Skin, White Masks* only gained recognition in the early 1980s, following the emergence of the academic field of postcolonialism.*

Criticism

When Frantz Fanon's *Black Skin, White Masks* was first published in 1952, it went largely unnoticed. Many people—including well-respected French academics like the historian Raoul Girardet* and the psychoanalyst Octave Mannoni*—were still in favor of colonialism.* They believed it was a way to overcome an "overpowering sense of national humiliation" following the Nazi* occupation of France.[1] Girardet remained a staunch supporter of French Algeria until the late 1960s. Referring to the year of the German invasion of France, he later wrote: "The background to the movement to resist [decolonization] was the effort to erase the memory of the 1940 defeat, which remained tragically present in the French consciousness."[2]

While the British historian Stephen Tyre notes that French anti-colonialist sentiment did emerge in the decade following World War II

> **❝** I find myself suddenly in the world and I recognize that I have one right alone: That of demanding human behavior from the other. One duty alone: That of not renouncing my freedom through my choices … I should constantly remind myself that the real leap consists in introducing invention into existence. In the world through which I travel, I am endlessly creating myself. **❞**
>
> Frantz Fanon, *Black Skin, White Masks*

among a small minority,[3] the majority of French-educated colonial peoples, including political representatives and teachers, were not concerned with independence. Their objective was to obtain the same rights as French citizens. For instance, the *Jeune Algérien* movement was founded to help Algeria modernize within the French nation.[4] The radical rhetoric of *Black Skin, White Masks* was at odds with these moderate ideas.

Two broad shifts changed the response to Fanon's ideas. First, his involvement with the pro-liberation movement in Algeria and the publication of his last work, *The Wretched of the Earth*, made him a household name among select groups of the French left. French intellectuals including the philosopher Jean-Paul Sartre,* the thinker Simone de Beauvoir* (a key figure in the history of the feminist movement), and the novelist and philosopher Albert Camus,* all cited Fanon.

Second, the decades following Fanon's death were much more in tune with his radical views. In the 1960s, citizens in the United States and Western Europe campaigned for racial and gender equality and better pay, while opposition mounted against their governments' participation in the Vietnam War* and against the development of nuclear weapons. In 1968, this unrest culminated in a series of riots in major cities like Newark, Watts, and Paris. In this context of skepticism, in which social habits and standards, and government and military institutions, were radically reassessed, Fanon's work found a new, and more receptive, audience.

Responses

Because Fanon's *Black Skin, White Masks* did not gain acclaim until after his death, he did not have a chance to respond to critics. However, in many ways he preempted their arguments. In the text he often makes use of Hegelian dialectic.* This form of discussion involves expressing an argument, providing the counterargument, and then reaching a conclusion—or "synthesis"—that seeks to reconcile the two. So Fanon incorporates opposing viewpoints into his work and demonstrates their shortcomings.

Fanon was a skillful critic of pro-colonialist views that predicted the enduring influence of colonialism* on decolonized countries. In the 1980s his ideas gained the attention of scholars of postcolonial studies—a field of inquiry that had emerged in response to shifting academic views on race and empire. Eurocentric* readings of cultures outside the West (that is, readings that assume the primacy of European culture and history) were now seen to be limited. As scholars explored the enduring effects of colonialism on culture, Fanon's work gained new meaning. Scholars questioned Western involvement in developing countries, and examined the extent of the West's self-interest. In this climate Fanon's work provided a useful frame of reference for understanding postcolonial society.

Fanon's ideas have proved particularly useful in the debate around the expansion of neoliberal* policies in Africa. Neoliberals argue that the state should play no part in economic matters; its role is to privatize public services and encourage free market trade. Opponents argue that in seeking to impose a specifically Western, capitalist ideology on developing countries, neoliberalism is not so different from colonialism. Fanon's work has also been used to discuss the effect of neoliberalism on postcolonial studies.[5]

Conflict and Consensus

Fanon's initial championing by French intellectuals, including the philosopher Jean-Paul Sartre, the thinker Simone de Beauvoir, and the novelist Albert Camus, helped introduce him to a much wider audience. Algeria's independence in 1962, which was followed by the decolonization of France's other territories, gave added weight to Fanon's writing. Indeed, the change in the public response and academic assessment of Fanon's work underscores how quickly cultural shifts can occur. From being an obscure and relatively unknown work in the 1950s, *Black Skin, White Masks* has become central to the field of postcolonial studies, global diaspora studies* and studies of countercultural resistance.* The emergence of disciplines that focus on understanding racial inequality, interracial violence and oppression, provided Fanon with a new audience.

Views about Fanon and his work have clearly transformed over time. Fanon was once deported from Algeria and forced to travel in secret. Yet today he is revered as the founding father of postcolonial studies and a central figure in the fight for decolonization. In this sense, his reputation is directly linked to the decolonization movement itself. This shift serves as a reminder that countercultural writing is typically met with resistance, but can come to be accepted as cultural and political norms change.

NOTES

1   Ian S. Lustick, "Wars of Position and Hegemonic Practice," *Unsettled States, Disputed Lands: Britain and Ireland, France and Algeria, Israel and the West Bank-Gaza* (New York: Cornell University Press, 1993), 152.

2   Raoul Girardet, *L'Idée Coloniale en France: 1871–1962* (Paris: Table Ronde, 1972), 248.

3   Stephen Tyre, "Historiography," *A Historical Companion to Postcolonial Literature*, ed. Prem Poddar et al (Edinburgh: Edinburgh University Press, 2008), 153.

4   Saliha Belmessous, *Assimilation and Empire: Uniformity in French and British Colonies*, 1541–1954 (Oxford: Oxford University Press, 2013), 159–60.

5   Neil Lazarus, *The Postcolonial Unconscious* (Cambridge: Cambridge University Press, 2011), 136–7.

MODULE 10
THE EVOLVING DEBATE

KEY POINTS

- Frantz Fanon's *Black Skin, White Masks* was an immensely important anti-colonialist* work. It helped pave the way for a number of academic fields of inquiry dedicated to the better understanding of race relations.

- Fanon's work was very much before its time. His influence is evident in the fields of Caribbean studies, postcolonial studies,* global diaspora studies,* and the study of literary resistance, counterculture and human rights.*

- These fields, which use his ideas about the role racism plays in a society's culture, only emerged several decades after his death.

Uses And Problems

Frantz Fanon's *Black Skin, White Masks* has proved an important text for several disciplines that emerged in the decades following decolonization.* These disciplines include postcolonialism, human rights studies and diaspora studies. Fanon's ideas have also played a key role in discussions about how race, sexual identity, and gender affect power relations. Fanon's writing about colonial racism* paved the way for later scholars to engage with the issue. Outside academia, Fanon has influenced a number of separatist* movements, including Pan-Africanism* (a movement aimed at creating solidarity between people of African ancestry, wherever they may live) and black nationalism* (a movement, often associated with the United States, with the aim of creating a society for black people independent from white society).

> **"** I, the man of color, want only this: That the tool never possess the man. That the enslavement of man by man cease forever. That is, of one by another. That it be possible for me to discover and to love man, wherever he may be. The Negro is not. Any more than the white man. **"**
>
> Frantz Fanon, *Black Skin, White Masks*

Fanon's work remains under-studied in France, largely due to enduring controversies over the country's colonial* past. Anglo-American scholars, however, have celebrated his contribution ever since the first English and Spanish translations of his work were published in 1967. These translations helped to introduce Fanon to a much wider audience. His books were warmly received by a number of US, South African and South American countercultural* movements.

In the United States, Fanon's writing became "essential reading for Black revolutionaries in America and profoundly influenced their thinking."[1] These revolutionaries included the militant Black Panther Party.* Fanon's influence on the Black Panthers has been the subject of much discussion. For example, when they were criticized for having a "fundamentally American outlook," the American academic Harold Cruse* countered by citing Fanon's popularity with the group. The American academics Floyd W. Hayes and Francis A. Kiene have noted that the party's platform and program drew heavily on Fanon's writings about the radical potential of the poorest black colonials.[2]

In South Africa, Fanon's work influenced the South African activist Stephen Bantu Biko,* who founded the Black Consciousness Movement* to fight apartheid.*[3] In Cuba, Fanon influenced the Marxist* revolutionary and military theorist Ernesto "Che" Guevara.*[4] In Bolivia, the radical writer Fausto Reinaga* (1906–94) cited Fanon's work in his seminal anti-colonialist and anti-assimilationist* book *The Indian Revolution* (1969). In the 1960s Fanon's ideas had an influence on radical politics across the developing world.[5]

Schools of Thought

The academic response to Fanon's work came slightly later than the political response. Initial critiques were largely confined to scholars of African studies.* In 1969 the British academic Martin Staniland examined Fanon's influence on African politics.[6] The Ghanaian scholar Emmanuel Hansen's 1974 article "Frantz Fanon: Portrait of a Revolutionary Intellectual," was a first attempt to understand Fanon's radicalism, and his role as a political theorist.*[7] In 1970 the British writer David Caute published a biography of Fanon, in which he used Fanon's ideas to discuss the dynamics of Cold War* conflict[8] (the Cold War was a period of tension between the Soviet Union and the United States, and nations aligned with each, that began after World War II and ended with the collapse of the Soviet Union in 1991).

The second "wave" of Fanon scholarship occurred in the 1980s, with the emergence of postcolonial studies. This field examines the enduring legacy of colonialism in culture, including literature, history, film, music, and visual art. Fanon's work influenced the Palestinian American writer Edward Said,* a leading postcolonial scholar.[9] Said took up Fanon's radical project, calling for both the colonized and colonizers to rethink their history. He wrote extensively on Fanon's work, contributing to a broader understanding of the origins of Fanon's Marxist thought.[10]

The Beninese philosopher P. Hountondji examined Fanon as part of a broader effort to dispel Western preconceptions about African philosophy. Hountondji argues that far from celebrating French Négritude,* Fanon dismissed the movement as acquiescing to colonial ideology. Hountondji says that the group essentially served as a forum in which black writers could write about black identity from within the colonialist framework.[11] In *Caribbean Discourse* (1989), the Martiniquan writer Edouard Glissant reads Fanon's efforts in Algeria as a response to the all-pervasiveness of colonial racism in Martinique and France—he argues that Fanon had to go where the mistreatment of blacks was explicit and visible in order to study its root causes. He could then find ways to contest black subjugation that could be applied to the much more subtle dynamics of racism in France. Glissant terms this approach "diversion."[12]

In Current Scholarship

As well as helping to shape African, postcolonial and diaspora studies, Fanon's ideas have played an important role in the field of human rights studies. His thinking has been used in examinations of race relations,* institutional racism* (that is, racism in organizations and bodies such as the police and the courts) and systemic violence and police brutality against black people in the United States. On these topics, the most noteworthy publications are *"Race," Writing, and Difference* (1989)[13] by the American academic H. L. Gates—which remains a seminal work in the study of how race relations are depicted in literature—and the South African-born academic D. T. Goldberg's *Anatomy of Racism* (1990).[14] The latter work builds on Fanon's ideas to explore how racism continues to inform contemporary culture, from our readings of history and applications of the law to workplace dynamics.

Another book that draws on Fanon's ideas is *Reading Rodney King/ Reading Urban Uprising*[15] by the American academic R. Gooding-Williams. This book was published in 1993. Two years earlier a black taxi driver, Rodney King, had been brutally attacked by white police officers. Four officers were charged with excessive use of force and assault with a deadly weapon, but after a three-month trial, in front of a predominantly white jury, they were acquitted. Their acquittal provoked riots across Los Angeles. Gooding-Williams examines the riots in relation to Fanon's ideas on interracial violence.

NOTES

1   Kathleen Neal Cleaver, "'Back to Africa': The Evolution of the International Section of the Black Panther Party (1969–1972)," in *The Black Panther Party (Reconsidered)*, ed. Charles Earl Jones (Baltimore, Maryland: Black Classic Press, 1998), 253.

2   Floyd W. Hayes and Francis A. Kiene, "'All Power to the People': The Political Thought of Huey P. Newton and the Black Panther Party" in *The Black Panther Party (Reconsidered)*, ed. Charles Earl Jones (Baltimore, Maryland: Black Classic Press, 1998), 160.

3   Reginald Nel, "Postcolonial missiology in the face of empire: in dialogue with Frantz Fanon and Steve Bantu Biko," *Studia Historiae Ecclesiasticae* 37, no. 3 (2011): 157–70, accessed August 10, 2015, http://hdl.handle.net/10500/5657.

4   Michael Löwy. *The Marxism of Che Guevara: Philosophy, Economics, Revolutionary Warfare* (Lanham, MD: Rowman & Littlefield, 1973), 73.

5   Jerome Branche, *Race, Colonialism and Social Transformation in Latin American and the Caribbean* (Gainesville, FL: University Press of Florida, 2008), 8.

6   Martin Staniland, "Frantz Fanon and the African Political Class," *African Affairs* vol. 68 (January 1969): 4–25.

7   Emmanuel Hansen, "Frantz Fanon: Portrait of a Revolutionary Intellectual," *Transition* 46 (1974): 25–36.

8   David Caute, *Frantz Fanon* (Michigan: Viking Press, 1970).

9   Edward Said, *Orientalism* (New York: Vintage, 1983); and *Culture and Imperialism* (London: Chatto and Windus, 1993).

10 Bill Ashcroft and Pal Ahluwalia, *Edward Said: The Paradox of Identity* (London: Routledge, 1999); and *Out of Africa: Post-Structuralism's Colonial Roots* (London and New York: Routledge, 2010).

11 P. Hountondji, *African Philosophy: Myth and Reality* (Bloomington: Indiana University Press, 1983), 24–5.

12 E. Glissant. *Caribbean Discourse*, trans. J. M. Dash (Charlottesville: University of Virginia Press, 1989), 23–6.

13 Henry Louis Gates. *"Race," Writing, and Difference* (Chicago: University of Chicago Press, 1989).

14 D. T. Goldberg, ed., *Anatomy of Racism* (Minneapolis: University of Minnesota Press, 1990).

15 See R. Gooding-Williams, "'Look, A Negro!'" in *Reading Rodney King/ Reading Urban Uprising* (New York: Routledge, 1993).

IMPACT AND INFLUENCE TODAY

KEY POINTS

- Frantz Fanon's *Black Skin, White Masks* remains an important critique of institutional racism* (racism in a nation's vital bodies and organizations—the courts, for example) and systems of oppression.

- Fanon's text highlights the insidiousness of racism and the extent to which it shapes views of black people in the West.

- *Black Skin, White Masks* provides an invaluable tool for understanding racism's role in power relations today and offers ideas about how to eradicate it.

Position

Frantz Fanon's *Black Skin, White Masks* has had an enduring and far-reaching impact that goes beyond discussions about colonialism:* Fanon's ideas are acutely relevant to cultural and race relations* today. Race and class inequality, cultural prejudice, and tensions between immigrants and native populations remain pressing concerns; and scholars apply Fanon's methodology to contemporary race relations in the United States.[1]

Ongoing controversies over acts of police brutality against black people in the US, and the high ratio of black youth in US prisons, for example, remind us that for many, the world has not really changed. Fanon's description of the way black people are demonized rings especially true in the light of killings of unarmed African American youths by white police officers who have then been acquitted. These killings have led to widespread protests, most notably in the city of

> **❝** According to Fanon, we must be aware of the inadequacy of academic discourse and analysis to fully comprehend the racial situation. Our academic understandings of race must be supplemented by experience in order to fully comprehend a given racial situation. **❞**
>
> Kelly Estrada and Peter McLaren, "A Dialogue on Multiculturalism and Democratic Culture"

Ferguson,* Missouri, in 2014. The black community's reaction to these events reflects long-standing resentment of a system that is seen to breed fear of, and hatred toward, black people. In turn, scholars have sought to apply Fanon's methodology to understand the politics of police brutality and the role it plays in racial oppression.[2]

Fanon's identification of the demonization of black people under colonialism also anticipates what critics refer to today as the prison industrial complex. This term links the rapid expansion of the US prison population to overlapping interests between prisons, business, and government, given that private companies build and supply prisons. The mass incarceration of black people also plays into the hands of a multi-billion dollar industry that uses cheap prison labor to manufacture products. This is not so different from the repressive experiences that black people endured under slavery.

Many of Fanon's arguments are also central to debates about the West's treatment of the developing world.* In the twenty-first century, as digital media and global corporations influence the language, culture, and thought of local communities, Fanon's recognition of the importance of local culture gains new meaning. Fanon shows that individual and collective autonomy* depend on communities resisting assimilation;* in order to retain their identities, they have to cultivate modes of thought that are independent from those imposed from above. In this context too, Fanon's work has much to offer.

Interaction

Fanon's ideas are now established. The system he was opposing no longer exists. As a result his work is now used mainly in discussions about racial inequality, or to discuss gender dynamics within human rights* movements.

Scholars have used Fanon's work to understand gender relations, both within systems of oppression and within countercultural* movements. Historically, movements against racial oppression have focused on the rights of *men*. This was true of the anti-colonialist* movement in France and its colonies and the American Civil Rights Movement.* For scholars who examine gender dynamics, Fanon is a useful source. His tendency to sideline women in his critique of racial oppression was symptomatic of tendencies in the wider world.

This discussion began in the early 1990s with the emergence of women's studies.* It has gained momentum in the last decade and a half. Important initial publications on the topic include articles by the American academics Qadri Ismail and Gwen Bergner, who both address the depiction of women in Fanon's *Black Skin, White Masks* and *The Wretched of the Earth* (1961).[3] Their work was followed by research by other American academics: E. Ann Kaplan's assessment of female objectification* in colonial culture and Marie-Chantal Kalisa's examination of gender politics in Fanon.[4]

Other discussions have addressed Fanon's unsympathetic analysis of the work of the Martiniquan writer Mayotte Capécia. His portrayal of Capécia's female protagonist in her book *Je suis Martiniquaise*, and his portrayal of Capécia herself, is misogynistic* (that is, it is evidence of deeply sexist assumptions).[5] Assessing Fanon's treatment of women and their role in colonial society sheds light on the issue of gender not only in African nationalist movements but in race relations globally. Scholars have pointed out the absence of women in Fanon's vision of a decolonized* future. They have also suggested ways in which current countercultural and human rights movements might increase their effectiveness, and extend their reach.

The Continuing Debate

As well as examining Fanon's depiction of women, scholars in the last decade and a half have revisited his assessment of interracial relationships, which has gained new importance with the growth of the field of gender studies* and the rise of the Lesbian Gay Bisexual and Transgender movement. Similarly, the growth of the academic discipline of queer theory* has given rise to new readings of Fanon's work.

Queer theory grew from the field of gender studies. Its central idea is that identities are not fixed. In that sense, our identities do not determine who we are. Queer theorists have examined Fanon's understanding of homosexuality as a "symptom" of colonial racism.[6] Their discussions address important questions such as the concept of masculinity under colonialism. They look at the enduring legacy of this concept and how it surfaces today in the relations between the West and postcolonial countries. They address the conflation of masculinity and power and explore the place of homosexuality in a system that equates heterosexuality and virility with authority.

Another important concept that has been addressed by queer theorists is the concept of emasculation. Scholars have considered how loss of power is seen as a form of castration, and how this concept has historically been played out in systems of oppression. Fanon discusses these ideas at length in his essays on interracial relationships.

NOTES

1   Jodo Costa Vargas and Joy A. James, "Refusing Blackness-as-Victimization: Trayvon Martin and the Black Cyborgs," *Pursuing Trayvon Martin: Historical Contexts and Contemporary Manifestations*, ed. George Yancy and Janine Jones (Plymouth: Lexington Books, 2013), 193–204.

2   Sundiata Keita Cha-Jua, "Ferguson, The Black Radical Tradition and the Path Forward," *The Black Scholar*, accessed August 10, 2015, http://www. theblackscholar.org/ferguson-the-black-radical-tradition-and-the-path-forward/: George Yancy, "Forms of Spatial and Textual Alienation: The Lived Experience of Philosophy as Occlusion." *Graduate Faculty Philosophy* 35, no. 1/2 (2014): 7–22.

3   Qadir Ismail, "'Boys will be boys': Gender and National Agency in Frantz Fanon and LTTE," *Economic and Political Weekly* 27, no. 31/32 (1992): 1677–9; and Gwen Bergner. "Who is That Masked Woman? The Role of Gender in Fanon's *Black Skin, White Masks*," PMLA 110, no. 1 (1995): 75–88.

4   E. Ann Kaplan, *Looking for the Other: Feminism, Film and the Imperial Gaze* (New York: Routledge, 1997); and Marie-Chantal Kalisa, "Black Women and Literature: Revisiting Frantz Fanon's Gender Politics," *The Literary Griot* 14, no. 1/2 (2002): 1–22.

5   See Madhu Dubey. "The 'True Lie' of the Nation: Fanon and Feminism," *Differences: A Journal of Feminist Cultural Studies* 10, no. 2 (1998): 1–29; Tracy Denean Sharpley-Whiting, *Frantz Fanon: Conflicts and Feminisms* (Lanham, Maryland: Rowman & Littlefield, 1998); Christiane Makward. *Mayotte Capécia: Ou, L'Aliénation Selon Fanon* (Paris: Karthala, 1999); David Macey. *Frantz Fanon: A Life* (London: Granta, 2000); Suzanne Gauch, "Fanon on the Surface," *Parallax* 8, no. 2 (2002): 116–28; and Linda Lane and Hauwa Mahdi, "Fanon Revisited: Race, Gender and Coloniality Vis-à-vis Skin Colour," *The Melanin Millennium: Skin Color as 21st Century International Discourse*, ed. Ronald E. Hall (Dordrecht: Springer Science + Business Media, 2013), 169–81.

6   See Kobena Mercer, *Decolonization and Disappointment: Reading Fanon's Sexual Politics* (London: Institute of Contemporary Arts and Institute of International Visual Arts, 1996); Ann Pellegrini, *Performance Anxieties: Staging Psychoanalysis, Staging Race* (New York: Routledge, 1997); Terry Goldie, "Saint Fanon and Homosexual Territory," *Frantz Fanon: Critical Perspectives*, ed. Anthony C. Alessandrini (London: Routledge, 1999), 77–88; Karen Lovaas, *LGBT Studies and Queer Theory: New Conflicts* (London: Routledge, 2013); Kara Keeling, "Looking for M–: Queer Temporality, Black Political Possibility and Poetry from the Future," *GLQ: A Journal of Lesbian and Gay Studies* 15, no.14 (2009): 565–82; Anthony C. Alessandrini, ed., *Frantz Fanon: Critical Perspectives* (London: Routledge, 1999); and Daniel Boyarin, Daniel Itzkovitz and Ann Pellegrini, eds. *Queer Theory and the Jewish Question* (New York: Columbia University Press, 2013).

MODULE 12
WHERE NEXT?

KEY POINTS

- Fanon's *Black Skin, White Masks* remains a canonical text in studies of colonial* oppression, countercultural* resistance, race relations,* and the global diaspora.*

- Fanon's ideas are acutely relevant in today's globalized,* post-digital world. They are a reminder of the need for communities to develop their own autonomous* cultures beyond that imposed by global corporations and media networks.

- Fanon's work is a challenge to racism of all forms. It sheds light on the insidious ways that racism can seep into culture.

Potential

Although the system of colonial subjugation* challenged by Frantz Fanon in *Black Skin, White Masks* no longer exists, the ideas he expresses remain relevant in debates about race relations. Fanon has also inspired the fields of postcolonial* and diaspora studies. One important discussion focuses on the contradiction of attempting to redress racial inequality and black oppression through theoretical frameworks developed by white Europeans. Another asks how Fanon's call for African and Afro-Caribbean nations to develop an autonomous identity can be reconciled with his own indebtedness to the European intellectual tradition. Are his arguments valid despite the fact that they draw inspiration from the work of white scholars? Does his use of European intellectual disciplines like psychoanalysis* and Marxism* contradict his separatist* ethos? And if they do, what might black intellectuals today do differently?

> **❝**The landing of the white man on Madagascar inflicted injury without measure. … It is of course obvious that the Malagasy [Madagascan people] can perfectly well tolerate the fact of not being a white man. A Malagasy is a Malagasy; or, rather, no, not he is a Malagasy but … in an absolute sense he 'lives' his Malagasyhood. If he is a Malagasy, it is because the white man has come. **❞**
>
> Frantz Fanon, *Black Skin, White Masks*

These questions are important. They are reminders of the enduring legacy of colonialism in the socioeconomic and political dynamics of the developing world. They are also reminders of the ongoing impact of colonialism on cultural identity and intellectual heritage. Scholars working in the fields of postcolonial studies, African studies,* diaspora studies and race relations continue to address these questions. The paradox of Fanon's immersion in the culture he criticizes is the topic of books such as *Challenging Euro-America's Politics of Identity* (2008) by the African American scholar Jorge Luis Andrade Fernandes, or the Iranian American scholar Hamid Dabashi's *Theology of Discontent* (1993). Fernandes reveals how Fanon's work can help decolonized* nations develop their own distinct intellectual and cultural frames of reference. Dabashi explores the intellectual formation of Iran's national Islamic ideology.

Future Directions

Traces of Fanon's ideas can also be found in contemporary discussions about ethnocentrism*—the tendency to believe that one's own cultural group is more important than any other—in popular culture. Fanon can also be discerned in debates about Western depictions of particular ethnicities and cultures. Moreover, his work is acutely important to any discussion about the enduring legacy of colonialism. A key debate is how the legacy of colonialism impacts the West's treatment of, and attitude toward, the developing world.*

Fanon argues that Europe sees the colonies as fundamentally backward. That idea is as relevant today as it was in 1952. However, this view of Africa has come under increasing scrutiny in debates about international development. To identify Africa as a site of squalor, disease, and savagery is to deny its true identity, and the diversity of its many nations.[1] This argument is heavily indebted to Fanon. It has now moved beyond academic discourse and into the public arena. For example, the American writers Trey Parker and Matt Stone openly criticize Western preconceptions about African culture in their religious musical satire *Book of Mormon* (2011). This is evidence of a cultural shift: Fanon's ideas are no longer controversial.

More evidence of this cultural shift can be seen in the criticism of the Western coverage of the Ebola* outbreak in West Africa in 2014–5. Critics noted that the coverage tended to present ignorant and hyperbolic views of the continent.[2] The underlying causes of the outbreak—health inequities in African countries—remained under-discussed. For Africa to gain true political and economic autonomy, the West must first encourage and support equal access to public health services.

As the Danish anthropologist Ruth J. Prince notes, the issue is inherently political, because science is supposed to be depoliticized; "science in the service of man … is often non-existent in the colonies."[3] This critique echoed earlier criticism of the media coverage of the AIDS* epidemic in the 1980s and a previous Ebola outbreak in the 1990s, which were coupled with public imagery of impoverished African nations, incapable of responding to these crises. Each of these calls for action drew on Fanon's argument that the former colonies need to develop an autonomous culture and plan for a postcolonial existence independent from European influence.

Summary

Frantz Fanon's *Black Skin, White Masks* (1952) remains a seminal work. Ahead of its time, it discussed issues that would remain a concern for human rights activists, scholars, politicians, and policy makers for the next 50 years: the underlying causes and long-term effects of colonial racism,* Western ethnocentrism, and racial oppression.

Fanon saw racism as a cultural construct: one embedded in social norms and passed on from generation to generation. This idea was an important contribution to the discussion of race relations in his time. It helped set the stage for later discussions about cultural development, heritage, and identity across a number of different disciplines. Certainly, disciplines that did not exist when Fanon was alive are heavily indebted to his ideas. His unique, cross-disciplinary approach to the idea of racial inequality, meanwhile, helped set a precedent for other scholarly writing.

Fanon's text is both a seminal work of scholarship and an intriguing piece of writing. His use of different theoretical concepts, and his impassioned, angry tone, make for a fascinating read. He shows how deeply racism is imbedded in systems of oppression. He also shows how useful racism can be in strengthening systems of power.

Fanon denounces oppressive regimes. He suggests ways the oppressed might reaffirm their autonomy. His work is an incitement to action as compelling today as when it was first published.

NOTES

1   C. Sargent and S Larchanché, "Disease, risk, and contagion: French colonial and postcolonial constructions of 'African' bodies," *J Bioeth Inquiry* 4 (December 2014): 455–66; S. Sastry and M. J. Dutta. "Postcolonial constructions of HIV/AIDS: meaning, culture, and structure," *Health Communication* 26, no. 5 (July-August 2011): 437–49.

2   Laura Seay and Kim Yi Dionne, "The long and ugly tradition of treating Africa as a dirty, diseased place," *Washington Post*, August 25, 2014, accessed August 10, 2015, http://www.washingtonpost.com/blogs/monkey-cage/wp/2014/08/25/othering-ebola-and-the-history-and-politics-of-pointing-at-immigrants-as-potential-disease-vectors/.

3   Ruth J. Prince, "Situating Health and the Public in Africa: Historical and Anthropological Perspectives," *Making and Unmaking Public Health in Africa: Ethnographic and Historical Perspectives*, ed. Ruth J. Prince and Rebecca Marsland (Athens, Ohio: Ohio University Press, 2014), 2–51.

GLOSSARY

GLOSSARY OF TERMS

African studies: a field of academic enquiry that examines the history, culture and politics of Africa and African identity, both within the continent and in relation to the rest of the world.

AIDS: acronym standing for acquired immune deficiency syndrome, caused by the human immunodeficiency virus (HIV), a disease that attacks sufferers' ability to fight off infections. The disease is thought to have originated in non-human primates (apes) in west-central Africa and to have spread to humans in the twentieth century, in line with the emergence of colonialism and the growth of large colonial African cities.

Algerian War (1954–62): a war waged by various anti-colonialist factions of the French colony of Algeria on France, in order to attain independence from French rule. It was among the most violent wars in both Algerian and French history, and remains a traumatic memory for both countries.

Alienation: refers to an individual's estrangement from his or her society, community or world. It is often referred to in relation to Karl Marx's theory of social alienation, which he saw as the consequence of living in a society divided into social classes in which wealth and power are distributed unevenly.

Allied powers: refers to France, the United Kingdom, the United States, and the USSR, which fought together during World War II to defeat Nazi Germany, Italy and Japan (known as the Axis powers).

American Civil War (1861–5): an armed conflict between the slave-owning states of the American South and the northern states, sparked by the secession of seven southern states in 1861.

Anthropology: the study of humans and human behavior, and their cultures. The field draws on a number of other fields in the physical, biological, social sciences and humanities.

Anti-colonialism: the critique of or opposition to the system of colonialism and colonial rule, either by the colonized or by external parties who view the system as socially or economical unjust.

Anti-psychiatry: the opposition to conventional psychiatric methods and treatments. It gained momentum in the 1960s, when political activists and scholars began to question standard definitions of mental illness.

Anti-Semitism: prejudice against, fear of, and discrimination against Jewish people based on their ethnicity, beliefs, or heritage.

Apartheid: a system of racial segregation in South Africa between 1948 and 1994, enforced through legislation. The system curtailed the rights, movement and associations of the non-white inhabitants of the country.

Autonomy: refers to the independence and freedom of either action or belief. An autonomous individual is one who can believe and act independently. An autonomous country is one that is socially, economically, and politically independent.

Avant-garde: generally refers to European art and literature produced in Zurich, Paris and Berlin between 1910 and World War II, including movements such as cubism, dada, and surrealism, which aimed to break with traditional conventions in art.

Black Consciousness Movement: an anti-Apartheid movement in South Africa that emerged in the 1960s to oppose discrimination against black South Africans.

Black nationalism: a movement that advocates black separatism from European society, self-sufficiency and race pride. The movement is generally associated with African Americans, and developed following the success of the Haitian Revolution of 1986.

Black Panther Party: a radical US socialist, black, nationalist group active between 1966 and 1982, which championed the use of violence to combat police brutality against blacks and *de facto* segregation.

Civil Rights Movement: a movement in the United States to secure equal rights for black people, outlaw segregation and remove discriminatory legislation against blacks. The movement gained sway in the mid-1950s but was at its most intense in the 1960s.

Cold War (1947–91): a period of intense military and political tension following World War II between Western powers (the United States and its NATO allies) and Eastern powers including the Soviet Union, East Germany and China. It ended in 1991 with the collapse of the Soviet Union.

Colonial racism: refers to discrimination against colonized people by their ruling power, generally based on the assumption that the ruled are inferior to their rulers.

Colonialism: refers to the rule of one country by another, involving unequal power relations between the ruler (colonist) and ruled (colony), and the exploitation of the colonies' resources to strengthen the economy of the colonizers' home country.

Communism: a socioeconomic system based on common ownership of both production methods and resources, and the outcomes of production (goods and services).

Countercultural resistance: any effort (such as a strike or protest) to oppose or criticize a dominant ideology, culture or system, either by pointing out the system's flaws or by offering an alternative.

Cross-disciplinary/interdisciplinary: the study of a problem, question or topic that combines different disciplines, schools of thought, or theoretical approaches.

Cubism: an early twentieth-century radical art movement that changed the course of European painting and sculpture. It is characterized by the depiction of objects from multiple perspectives.

Cultural assimilation/assimilationism: the policy of encouraging a community to take on the ideology, values, language and tastes of another, often at the expense of their own, and with a view to making them more submissive.

Cultural studies: an academic field that examines cultural phenomena such as class structure, ideology, national formations, gender, sexuality and perceptions of ethnicity through a number of different theoretical approaches, including anthropology, political science, and sociology. The study is based on the assumption that culture is not fixed.

Dada: an early twentieth-century countercultural art movement in Zurich, Berlin, New York and Paris that emerged in response to the outbreak of World War I. Many dadaists believed the war to have been a result of the "reason" and "logic" of capitalist society.

Dehumanization: the systematic process of demonizing another person or persons by making them appear less than human, and therefore not deserving of humane treatment.

Developing world: a term used to define impoverished nations in Africa, the Middle East and Asia. The term gained use in the early 1990s, replacing "Third World" due to the latter's negative and hierarchical connotations.

Diaspora studies: the academic study of dispersed ethnic populations (diaspora). The field examines questions such as the reason for their resettlement, their acclimatization to their new context, and the relationship between them and the local community.

Ebola virus: a viral disease that started in Sub-Saharan Africa. It was first identified in 1976, when it infected 284 people in Sudan and killed 151. During an outbreak in 2014–15 in West Africa, the virus killed over 11,000 people, leading to widespread fears about its potential spread across the globe.

Economics: an academic field that examines economic systems, structures, policies, and trends and their influence on the production, distribution, and consumption of goods and services.

El Moudjahid: an Algerian newspaper written in French. It was conceived by the FLN during the Algerian War to aid Algeria's struggle for independence from French colonial rule. The name is a French transliteration of the Arabic word *mujahid*, which means "holy warrior."

Emancipation: the procurement of social, economic, and/or political rights or equality by a previously disenfranchised group.

Ethnocentrism: refers to the tendency to believe that one's own ethnic or cultural group is more important, or central, than others. In scholarship, an ethnocentric study would be one that privileges the scholar's culture over others.

Eurocentrism: a form of ethnocentrism that sees European culture as superior to or more important than other cultures, or any act of interpretation that assumes a European perspective without acknowledging others.

Existential humanism: a branch of philosophy that places emphasis on the human subject. It views human experience as a process of self-understanding and self-knowledge.

Existentialism: a branch of philosophy dealing with matters of human existence, which argues (roughly) that individuals develop through exercising their own free will.

Ferguson riots (2014): a series of public protests that took place in Ferguson, Missouri and surrounding areas following the acquittal of the white police officer responsible for the shooting of the black eighteen-year-old youth Michael Brown. The riots were held to protest against the US police force's perceived legacy of brutality against the black community, especially black males.

First person: a narrative mode in which the protagonist (main character) is referred to by the first-person pronouns "I," "me," and "us." It is often used to create empathy in the reader, or to increase a sense of closeness to the narrated events.

French Union: France as it was known between 1946 and 1958, immediately following the dismantling of the French Empire—the old French colonial system—and just before the decolonization of the last French colonies (Cambodia, South Vietnam, Morocco, Tunisia, and Laos).

***Front de Libération Nationale* /National Liberation Front (FLN):** an Algerian socialist political party. It was founded in 1954 to help the country gain independence France.

Gender relations: refers to any interaction between the two genders based on the social roles designated to each one.

Gender studies: the interdisciplinary academic study of gender relations, gender identity, and sexual orientation, including how gender and sexual orientation are perceived and/or represented in culture.

Globalization: the process of integration and interaction among the governments, peoples, and companies of different countries. The process is fuelled by international trade and investment, and propelled by information technology.

Harlem Renaissance: a movement begun in the 1920s by black artists and writers in New York city to celebrate black identity and explore black alienation in American culture.

Hegelian dialectics: a form of philosophical discussion that involves putting forth one's argument (thesis), providing the counterargument (antithesis), and then reaching a conclusion—or "synthesis"—that seeks to reconcile the two.

Holocaust: refers to the state-sponsored genocide of six million Jewish people in Europe by Nazi Germany and its collaborators during World War II. The process was designed to "cleanse" humanity of its lesser ethnicities, leaving only the Aryan race.

Homophobia: refers to the hatred or fear of homosexuals, and any behavior or treatment of homosexuals based on the assumption that homosexuality is unnatural, or inferior to, heterosexuality.

Human rights studies: an academic field that examines the evolution of the principles and norms used to ascribe liberties and rights to citizens.

Indochina War (1946–54): also known as the First Indochina War and in contemporary Vietnam as the Anti-French Resistance War, this was a conflict between French Indochina and its colonial ruler, France, that resulted in North Vietnam's independence.

Institutional racism: racist discrimination by any system or institution, including schools, hospitals, or even government.

Lacanian psychoanalysis: a branch of psychoanalysis founded by Jacques Lacan (1901–81) that challenges and builds on the ideas of traditional Freudian psychoanalysis. Lacan was interested in how identity helps to structure human experience. He explored how identity develops, looking at the role of language, culture, social structure, and family; he considered language to be the most important of these.

Literary criticism: the evaluation, study, and interpretation of literature.

Marxism: a field of study based on the work of the German political theorist and philosopher Karl Marx (1818–83). It investigates the role of class struggle and social inequality in culture, economics, politics, and history.

Mirror stage: a concept developed by the French psychoanalyst Jacques Lacan, based on the view that infants first develop a sense of identity through the perception of themselves as seen from the outside. The first time a child recognizes their reflection is also the first time they perceive themselves as individual subjects. Relatedly, infants develop their identity comparatively—that is, through self-comparison with other people. Fanon builds on these ideas to argue that black children learn early on to identify as white, and therefore to be effectively blind to their own blackness.

Misogyny: refers to the dislike or hatred of women, and behavior that reflects that hatred, including sexual discrimination against women, violence, denigration, and the treatment of women as passive objects (also known as objectification).

Mythology: refers to either a culture's collected stories that explain their customs, history, or fundamental beliefs, or the study of these myths.

Narrative perspective: refers to the narrator's position with regards to his/her story. Depending on their perspective, they will have more or less insight into the behavior of the characters involved, and they will manifest more or less bias.

Nazi Party: the ruling party of Germany between 1934 and 1945, also known as the Third Reich. Nazi ideology was essentially fascist, and incorporated anti-Semitism and scientific racism.

Négritude: a literary movement from the 1930s to the late 1950s, begun by African and Caribbean writers living in Paris, to protest against French colonial rule and French cultural assimilation.

Negrophobia: a (now outdated) term used to describe the hatred or fear of black people, and any behavior based on that fear. It is similar to racism, with the significant difference that a black person can feel it towards themselves or toward other blacks.

Neoliberalism: a set of economic policies that supports and encourages economic liberalization, free trade, open markets, the privatization of public services, deregulation of markets, and the growth of the role of the private sector.

Nuremberg Trials (1945–49): a series of 13 trials held in Nuremberg, Germany after World War II to bring Nazi criminals to justice. The trials revealed the extent of the Jewish genocide known as the Holocaust.

Objectification: a philosophical term that refers to any instance in which a person is treated as a thing.

Pan-Africanism: a movement and ideology aimed at creating global solidarity among Africans. The movement is based on the idea that economic, political and social progress are dependent on unity; to unify Africans worldwide is the first step towards their political and economic emancipation from the West.

Paris Massacre (1961): a violent massacre that took place at the tail end of the Algerian War (1954–62). The French National Police attacked 30,000 Algerian pro-National Liberation Front (FLN) demonstrators. Evidence suggests that the massacre was intentional, and designed to suppress Algeria's efforts to gain independence. The exact number of deaths remains contested.

Pathology: a broad term for any psychological or physical medical disorder or suffering. Pathological behavior refers to behavior that reflects an underlying mental disorder.

Phenomenology: in philosophy, this is the study of the structures that inform our experience and our consciousness. In psychology, it is the study of subjective experience.

Philosophy: a field of the humanities that studies fundamental human problems related to reality, knowledge, existence, reason, language, and values.

Political science: a field of the social sciences that examines government policies and politics, and the dynamics of nation, government, and state.

Postcolonialism/postcolonial studies: an academic discipline that examines the legacies of imperial and colonial rule, including the effect of these on the culture of the colonized as well as the depiction of the colonized in the art, film, and literature produced by the colonists themselves.

Power relations: a term used to refer to the (often unequal) division of power between the genders, races, social classes or nations, and how that division shapes culture. A discussion of power relations between a colonial ruler and subject, for instance, would examine how the unequal distribution of power in the colonies results in the erasure of the native culture.

Psychiatry: the branch of medicine that deals in the study, treatment, and prevention of medical disorders.

Psychology: an academic and applied discipline concerning the study and treatment of mental behavior and mental functions.

Psychopathology: refers to the manifestation of mental illness or distress, or of behaviors or events indicative of mental impairment.

Queer theory: a broad field of poststructuralist theory associated with both lesbian, gay, bisexual and transgender (LGBT) studies and women's studies, concerned with enquiry into both what is considered "normal" and supposedly deviant identity categories.

Race relations: refers to the economic, social, and political dynamics between ethnicities and races, and any inequalities, tensions, or conflicts that might arise therein.

Racial discrimination: refers to any individual or collective act based on the assumption that one race is superior to another. This might include a law that favors one race over another, or an individual's treatment of a person based on their race.

Racial prejudice: refers to the prejudgment or the formation of preconceived notions about a person or persons based on their race or ethnicity. These beliefs are generally unfounded and not based on actual experience or knowledge.

Racial tension: refers to any conflict or problem between different races or ethnicities resulting from imbalances of power or underlying assumptions about the superiority of one race over the other.

Racism: refers to both discrimination and prejudice based on the perception of biological differences between people, including race and ethnicity. Racism can include both intentional discriminatory treatment and unintentional discrimination, regardless of whether the behavior was intended to harm.

Second person: a narrative mode in which the protagonist is referred to by the second-person pronoun "you." It is rarely used in fiction as it is generally considered difficult to sustain.

Separatism: a term used for the advocacy of ethnic, racial, gender, cultural, tribal, governmental or religious separation from a larger group, as a means to obtain autonomy.

Socialism: an economic and social system in which the means of production are shared rather than privately owned. In political science, socialist theory refers to work aimed at promoting, or bringing about, the establishment of a socialist system.

Sociology: the academic study of social behavior. The discipline examines the origins and development of social relations, their different modes of organization, and different social institutions.

Stream-of-conscious narration: refers to a type of narration that depicts multiple simultaneous thoughts and feelings with a view to reflecting the interior workings of the mind.

Subjugation: refers to the conquering of, or gaining control of, someone or something and rendering them subordinate.

Surrealism: a countercultural artistic movement born in early twentieth-century Paris as a reaction to the flattening effects of commodity culture, and, in particular, to the commodification of art.

Third person: a narrative mode in which the protagonist or main character is referred to with third person pronouns such as "he," "she" or "they."

Vichy France: The government in France between 1940 and 1944, during World War II, which supported the Axis powers of Germany, Japan, and Italy.

Vietnam War (1955–75): a Cold War-era conflict fought in Laos, Cambodia and Vietnam from 1955 to 1975 between North Vietnam and South Vietnam. The North Vietnamese saw the conflict as essentially a colonial one, and argued that the United States and France's role in South Vietnam made it a puppet state.

Women's rights movement: a series of efforts to attain rights for women equal to those of men.

World literature: refers to the circulation and study of literary works beyond their country of origin. It is often thought of by scholars as the natural successor to postcolonialism, allowing the examination of cultural difference to move beyond the interrogation of countries' power relations.

PEOPLE MENTIONED IN THE TEXT

Simone de Beauvoir (1908–86) was perhaps the most famous, and influential, feminist philosopher and writer of the twentieth century. Together with Jean-Paul Sartre, she played an important role in introducing Fanon to white intellectuals.

Albert Camus (1913–60) was a French novelist, existentialist philosopher, and journalist, and was awarded the Nobel Prize for Literature in 1957. He was a huge proponent of Fanon's work, and a staunch opponent of French rule in Algeria.

Mayotte Capécia (1916–55) was a French Martiniquan writer known for the memoirs of her life in Paris, relationship with a white Parisian doctor, and subsequent treatment by the Parisian élite.

Aimé Césaire (1913–2008) was a French-speaking Martiniquan poet, novelist, and politician closely associated with the Négritude movement of the 1930s, '40s and '50s, and a friend and mentor to Fanon.

Ernesto "Che" Guevara (1928–67) was an Argentinian Marxist writer, revolutionary, physician and guerilla leader. He was a major figure in the Cuban Revolution, and has since become a symbol of countercultural resistance and revolution.

Harold Cruse (1916–2005) was an African American scholar and vocal social critic. He is best remembered for his book *The Crisis of the Negro Intellectual* (1967), and as one of the first professors of African-American studies, a field that only emerged in the very late 1960s.

Léon Damas (1912–78) was a French Martiniquan politician and poet, and one of the founders of the Négritude movement.

Raoul Girardet (1917–2013) was a French historian specializing in the history of military rule and French nationalism. Like other historians of his time, Girardet was initially a vocal proponent of colonialism and linked France's colonial history to its economic successes. His opinion shifted in the late 1960s following the Algerian War. His best-known work, *L'Idée Coloniale en France de 1871 à 1962* (1971), reflects this later anti-colonialist stance.

Martin Luther King, Jr. (1929–68) was an African American political activist and reverend, and the leader of the American Civil Rights movement until his assassination in 1968.

Jacques Lacan (1901–81) was a French psychoanalyst and psychiatrist best known for his development of Lacanian psychoanalysis, which had a profound influence on French philosophy and feminist theory.

Octave Mannoni (1899–1989) was a French writer and psychoanalyst who spent the first half of his adult life in Madagascar. He is best known for his book *Prospero and Caliban: The Psychology of Colonization* (1956), which Fanon and other black writers criticized as both short-sighted and racist.

Karl Marx (1818–83) was a German political philosopher and economist whose analysis of class relations under capitalism, and articulation of a more egalitarian system, provided the basis for communism.

Marcel Merleau-Ponty (1908–61) was a French phenomenological philosopher and writer, and the only major philosopher of his time to incorporate descriptive psychology in his work.

Kwame Nkrumah (1909–72) was the leader of the Gold Coast's fight for independence from British colonialism in 1957, after which he became the first president and prime minister of Ghana.

Fausto Reinaga (1906–94) was a Bolivian indigenous intellectual and writer, and a leading critic of the policy of cultural assimilation in India during British colonialism. He is best known for his articulation of this in *The Indian Revolution* (1969).

Jean-Paul Sartre (1905–80) was a French existential philosopher, and a leading thinker in the schools of twentieth-century French philosophy and Marxism. He was also a leading figure in Algeria's fight for independence from French rule, and responsible for introducing French Négritude, and Frantz Fanon's work, to white audiences in France.

Edward Said (1935–2003) was a Palestinian American writer, cultural critic, and theorist who helped found the field of postcolonial studies. He is best known for his books *Orientalism* (1978) and *Culture and Imperialism* (1993), both of which applied and engaged with Fanon's ideas.

Alfred Sauvy (1898–1990) was a French historian, demographer and anthropologist best known for coining the term "Third World" in 1952 to define countries unaligned with either the capitalist NATO bloc or the communist Soviet bloc. Sauvy defined these countries in terms of their poverty and exploitation by the United States, France, Soviet Union and China.

Léopold Sédar Senghor (1906–2001) was a Senegalese poet, cultural theorist and politician. As well as a founder of the Négritude movement, he was Senegal's first president (1960–80).

François Tosquelles (1912–94) was a Catalan psychiatrist, and is credited with helping establish institutional psychotherapy. Fanon's ideas were shaped by Tosquelles' identification of the impact of culture on psychopathological conditions.

Malcolm X (1925–65) was an African American human rights activist and Muslim minister, and a leading proponent of black separatism and critic of the Civil Rights Movement's advocation of racial integration. His championing of violence and his espousing of black supremacy were inspired by Fanon's ideas.

WORKS CITED

WORKS CITED

Ahluwalia, Pal. *Out of Africa: Post-Structuralism's* Colonial Roots. London and New York: Routledge, 2010.

Alessandrini, Anthony C., ed. *Frantz Fanon: Critical Perspectives.* London: Routledge, 1999.

Ashcroft, Bill and Pal Ahluwalia. *Edward Said: The Paradox of Identity.* London: Routledge, 1999.

Belmessous, Saliha. *Assimilation and Empire: Uniformity in French and British Colonies*, 1541–1954. Oxford: Oxford University Press, 2013.

Bergner, Gwen. "Who Is That Masked Woman? or, The Role of Gender in Fanon's Black Skin, White Masks," *PMLA* 110, no. 1 (1995): 75–88.

Boyarin, Daniel, Daniel Itzkovitz and Ann Pellegrini, ed. *Queer Theory and the Jewish Question.* New York: Columbia University Press, 2013.

Boyce Davies, Carol Elizabeth, ed. *Encyclopedia of the Global Diaspora Experience*, Vol. II. Santa Barbara. ABC-CLIO, 2008.

Branche, Jerome. *Race, Colonialism and Social Transformation in Latin America and the Caribbean*. Gainesville, FL: University Press of Florida, 2008.

Bulhan Abdilahi, Hussein. *Frantz Fanon and the Psychology of Oppression*. New York: Plenum Press, 1985.

Capécia, Mayotte, *Je suis Martiniquaise*. Paris: Corréa, 1948.

Caute, David. *Frantz Fanon*. New York: The Viking Press, 1970.

Césaire, Aimé and nine other writers. "Homage to Frantz Fanon." *Presence Africaine* 12 (1962): 130–52.

Cha-Jua, Sundiata Keita. "Ferguson, The Black Radical Tradition and the Path Forward." *The Black Scholar*. Accessed August 10, 2015. http://www.theblackscholar.org/ferguson-the-black-radical-tradition-and-the-path-forward/.

Cleaver, Kathleen Neal. "The Evolution of the International Section of the Black Panther Party (1969–1972)." *In The Black Panther Party (Reconsidered)*, edited by Charles Earl Jones, 211156. Baltimore, Maryland: Black Classic Press, 1998.

Dollimore, Jonathan. *Sexual Dissidence: Augustine to Wilde, Freud to Foucault*. Oxford: Oxford Paperbacks, 1991.

Dubey, Madhu. "The 'True Lie' of the Nation: Fanon and Feminism." *Differences: A Journal of Feminist Cultural Studies* 10, no. 2 (1998): 1–29.

Fanon, Frantz. *Black Skin, White Masks*, translated by Charles Lam Markmann. London: Pluto Press, 1986.

The Wretched of the Earth, translated by Constance Farrington. London: Penguin, 2001.

Friedman, David M. *A Mind of its Own: A Cultural History of the Penis*. New York: Simon and Schuster, 2001.

Fuss, Diana. "Interior Colonies: Frantz Fanon and the Politics of Identification." *Diacritics* 24, no 2/3 (1994): 20–42.

Gates, Henry Louis. "Critical Fanonism." *Critical Inquiry* 17, no. 3 (1992): 457–70.

Gates, Henry Louis, ed. *"Race," Writing, and Difference*. Chicago: University of Chicago Press, 1989.

Gauch, Suzanne. "Fanon on the Surface." *Parallax* 8, no. 2 (2002): 116–28.

Girardet, Raoul. *L'Idée Coloniale en France: 1871–1962*. Paris: Table Ronde, 1972.

Glissant, Edouard. *Caribbean Discourse*. Translated by J. M. Dash. Charlottesville: University of Virginia Press, 1989.

Goldberg, D. T., ed. *Anatomy of Racism*. Minneapolis: University of Minnesota Press, 1990.

Goldie, Terry. "Saint Fanon and Homosexual Territory." In *Frantz Fanon: Critical Perspectives*, edited by Anthony C. Alessandrini, 77–88. London: Routledge, 1999.

Gooding-Williams, R. "Look, A Negro!" In *Reading Rodney King/Reading Urban Uprising*, edited by R. Gooding Williams. New York: Routledge, 1993.

Hall, Stuart. "Cultural Identity and Diaspora." In *Identity: Community, Culture, Difference*, edited by J. Rutherford. London: Lawrence & Wishart, 1990.

"Negotiating Caribbean Identities." *New Left Review* 209 (1995): 3–14.

Hansen, Emmanuel. "Frantz Fanon: Portrait of a Revolutionary Intellectual." *Transition* 46 (1974): 25–36.

Hayes, Floyd W. and Francis A. Kiene. "'All Power to the People': The Political Thought of Huey P. Newton and the Black Panther Party." In *The Black Panther Party (Reconsidered)*, edited by Charles Earl Jones, 157–76. Baltimore, Maryland: Black Classic Press, 1998.

Hountondji, P. *African Philosophy: Myth and Reality*. Bloomington: Indiana University Press, 1983.

Ismail, Qadri. "'Boys will be boys': Gender and National Agency in Frantz Fanon and LTTE." *Economic and Political Weekly* 27, no 31/32 (1992): 1677–79.

Kalisa, Marie-Chantal. "Black Women and Literature: Revisiting Frantz Fanon's Gender Politics." *The Literary Griot* 14, no 1/2 (2002): 1–22.

Kaplan, E. Ann. *Looking for the Other: Feminism, Film and the Imperial Gaze.* New York: Routledge, 1997.

Keeling, Kara. "Looking for M–: Queer Temporality, Black Political Possibility and Poetry from the Future." *GLQ: A Journal of Lesbian and Gay Studies* 15, no. 4 (2009): 565–82.

LaGuerre, J. G. *Enemies of Empire.* St Augustine: University of the West Indies, 1984.

Lane, Linda and Hauwa Mahdi. "Fanon Revisited: Race Gender and Coloniality Vis-à vis Skin Colour." In *The Melanin Millennium: Skin Color as 21st Century International Discourse*, edited by Ronald E. Hall, 169–81. Dordrecht: Springer Science + Business Media, 2013.

Lazarus, Neil. *Resistance in Postcolonial African Fiction.* New Haven, CT: Yale University Press, 1990.

The Postcolonial Unconscious. Cambridge: Cambridge University Press, 2011.

Lewis, Melvin E. "Once I was a Panther." *Black American Literature Forum* 24, no. 3 (1990): 534–8.

Lovaas, Karen. *LGBT Studies and Queer Theory: New Conflicts, Collaborations and Contested Terrain.* Philadelphia: Howarth Press, 2006.

Löwy, Michael. *The Marxism of Che Guevara: Philosophy, Economics, Revolutionary Warfare.* Lanham, MD: Rowman & Littlefield, 1973.

Lustick, Ian S. "Wars of Position and Hegemonic Practice." In *Unsettled States, Disputed Lands: Britain and Ireland, France and Algeria, Israel and the West Bank-Gaza.* New York: Cornell University Press, 1993.

Macey, David. *Frantz Fanon: A Life.* London: Granta, 2000.

"Frantz Fanon, or the Difficulty of Being Martinican," *History Workshop Journal* 58, no. 3 (2004): 211–23.

Makward, Christiane. *Mayotte Capécia: Ou, L'Aliénation Selon Fanon.* Paris: Karthala, 1999.

Mercer, Kobena. "Decolonization and Disappointment: Reading Fanon's Sexual Politics." In *The Fact of Blackness: Frantz Fanon and Visual Representation*, edited by Alan Read. London: Institute of Contemporary Arts and Institute of International Visual Arts, 1996.

Nel, Reginald. "Postcolonial missiology in the face of empire: in dialogue with Frantz Fanon and Steve Bantu Biko." *Studia Historiae Ecclesiasticae* 37, no. 3 (2011): 157–70. Accessed August 10, 2015. http://hdl.handle.net/10500/5657.

Nursey-Bray, Paul. "Race and Nation: Ideology in the Thought of Frantz Fanon." *The Journal of Modern African Studies* 18, no. 1 (1980): 135–42.

Parry, Benita. "Liberation Theory: Variations on Themes of Marxism and Modernity." In *Postcolonial Studies: A Materialist Critique,* 75–92. London: Routledge, 2004.

Pellegrini, Ann. *Performance Anxieties: Staging Psychoanalysis, Staging Race.* New York: Routledge, 1997.

Prince, Ruth J. "Situating Health and the Public in Africa: Historical and Anthropological Perspectives." In *Making and Unmaking Public Health in Africa: Ethnographic and Historical Perspectives*, edited by Ruth J. Prince and Rebecca Marsland, 2–51. Athens, Ohio: Ohio University Press, 2014.

Said, Edward. *Orientalism.* New York: Vintage, 1983.

Culture and Imperialism. London: Chatto and Windus, 1993.

Sartre, Jean-Paul. Preface to *The Wretched of the Earth* by Frantz Fanon. Translated by Constance Farrington. New York and London: Penguin, 2001.

Anti-Semite and Jew: An Exploration of the Etiology of Hate. Translated by George J. Becker. New York: Schocken Books, 1995 [1946].

"Orphée Noir." In *Anthologie de la Nouvelle Poésie Négre et Malgache de Langue Française* by Leopold Senghor. Paris: Presses Universitaires de France, 2011.

Sargent, C. and S. Larchanché. "Disease, risk, and contagion: French colonial and postcolonial constructions of 'African' bodies." *J Bioeth Inquiry* 4, no. 8 (December 2014): 455–66.

Sastry, S. and M. J. Dutta. "Postcolonial constructions of HIV/AIDS: meaning, culture, and structure." *Health Commun* 26, no. 5 (July-August 2011): 437–49.

Seay, Laura and Kim Yi Dionne. '"The long and ugly tradition of treating Africa as a dirty, diseased place." *Washington Post*, August 25, 2014.

Sharpley-Whiting, Tracy Denean. *Frantz Fanon: Conflicts and Feminisms.* Lanham, Maryland: Rowman & Littlefield, 1998.

Shatz, Adam. "Frantz Fanon: The Doctor Prescribed Violence." *New York Times*, September 2, 2001. Accessed August 10, 2015. http://www.nytimes.com/2001/09/02/books/review/02SHATZTW.html.

Silverman, Max, ed. *Frantz Fanon's Black Skin, White Masks: New Interdisciplinary Essays*. Manchester: Manchester University Press, 2005.

Staniland, Martin. "Frantz Fanon and the African Political Class." *African Affairs* 68, no. 1 (1969): 4–25.

Tyre, Stephen. "Historiography." In *A Historical Companion to Postcolonial Literatures, Continental Europe and its Empires*, edited by Prem Poddar, Rajeev S. Patke, and Lars Jensen, 155–7. Edinburgh: Edinburgh University Press, 2008.

Yancy, George. "Forms of Spatial and Textual Alienation: The Lived Experience of Philosophy as Occlusion." *Graduate Faculty Philosophy* 35, no. 1/2 (2014): 7–22.

THE MACAT LIBRARY
BY DISCIPLINE

AFRICANA STUDIES

Chinua Achebe's *An Image of Africa: Racism in Conrad's Heart of Darkness*
W. E. B. Du Bois's *The Souls of Black Folk*
Zora Neale Huston's *Characteristics of Negro Expression*
Martin Luther King Jr's *Why We Can't Wait*
Toni Morrison's *Playing in the Dark: Whiteness in the American Literary Imagination*

ANTHROPOLOGY

Arjun Appadurai's *Modernity at Large: Cultural Dimensions of Globalisation*
Philippe Ariès's *Centuries of Childhood*
Franz Boas's *Race, Language and Culture*
Kim Chan & Renée Mauborgne's *Blue Ocean Strategy*
Jared Diamond's *Guns, Germs & Steel: the Fate of Human Societies*
Jared Diamond's *Collapse: How Societies Choose to Fail or Survive*
E. E. Evans-Pritchard's *Witchcraft, Oracles and Magic Among the Azande*
James Ferguson's *The Anti-Politics Machine*
Clifford Geertz's *The Interpretation of Cultures*
David Graeber's *Debt: the First 5000 Years*
Karen Ho's *Liquidated: An Ethnography of Wall Street*
Geert Hofstede's *Culture's Consequences: Comparing Values, Behaviors, Institutes and Organizations across Nations*
Claude Lévi-Strauss's *Structural Anthropology*
Jay Macleod's *Ain't No Makin' It: Aspirations and Attainment in a Low-income Neighborhood*
Saba Mahmood's *The Politics of Piety: The Islamic Revival and the Feminist Subject*
Marcel Mauss's *The Gift*

BUSINESS

Jean Lave & Etienne Wenger's *Situated Learning*
Theodore Levitt's *Marketing Myopia*
Burton G. Malkiel's *A Random Walk Down Wall Street*
Douglas McGregor's *The Human Side of Enterprise*
Michael Porter's *Competitive Strategy: Creating and Sustaining Superior Performance*
John Kotter's *Leading Change*
C. K. Prahalad & Gary Hamel's *The Core Competence of the Corporation*

CRIMINOLOGY

Michelle Alexander's *The New Jim Crow: Mass Incarceration in the Age of Colorblindness*
Michael R. Gottfredson & Travis Hirschi's *A General Theory of Crime*
Richard Herrnstein & Charles A. Murray's *The Bell Curve: Intelligence and Class Structure in American Life*
Elizabeth Loftus's *Eyewitness Testimony*
Jay Macleod's *Ain't No Makin' It: Aspirations and Attainment in a Low-Income Neighborhood*
Philip Zimbardo's *The Lucifer Effect*

ECONOMICS

Janet Abu-Lughod's *Before European Hegemony*
Ha-Joon Chang's *Kicking Away the Ladder*
David Brion Davis's *The Problem of Slavery in the Age of Revolution*
Milton Friedman's *The Role of Monetary Policy*
Milton Friedman's *Capitalism and Freedom*
David Graeber's *Debt: the First 5000 Years*
Friedrich Hayek's *The Road to Serfdom*
Karen Ho's *Liquidated: An Ethnography of Wall Street*

The Macat Library By Discipline

John Maynard Keynes's *The General Theory of Employment, Interest and Money*
Charles P. Kindleberger's *Manias, Panics and Crashes*
Robert Lucas's *Why Doesn't Capital Flow from Rich to Poor Countries?*
Burton G. Malkiel's *A Random Walk Down Wall Street*
Thomas Robert Malthus's *An Essay on the Principle of Population*
Karl Marx's *Capital*
Thomas Piketty's *Capital in the Twenty-First Century*
Amartya Sen's *Development as Freedom*
Adam Smith's *The Wealth of Nations*
Nassim Nicholas Taleb's *The Black Swan: The Impact of the Highly Improbable*
Amos Tversky's & Daniel Kahneman's *Judgment under Uncertainty: Heuristics and Biases*
Mahbub Ul Haq's *Reflections on Human Development*
Max Weber's *The Protestant Ethic and the Spirit of Capitalism*

FEMINISM AND GENDER STUDIES

Judith Butler's *Gender Trouble*
Simone De Beauvoir's *The Second Sex*
Michel Foucault's *History of Sexuality*
Betty Friedan's *The Feminine Mystique*
Saba Mahmood's *The Politics of Piety: The Islamic Revival and the Feminist Subject*
Joan Wallach Scott's *Gender and the Politics of History*
Mary Wollstonecraft's *A Vindication of the Rights of Woman*
Virginia Woolf's *A Room of One's Own*

GEOGRAPHY

The Brundtland Report's *Our Common Future*
Rachel Carson's *Silent Spring*
Charles Darwin's *On the Origin of Species*
James Ferguson's *The Anti-Politics Machine*
Jane Jacobs's *The Death and Life of Great American Cities*
James Lovelock's *Gaia: A New Look at Life on Earth*
Amartya Sen's *Development as Freedom*
Mathis Wackernagel & William Rees's *Our Ecological Footprint*

HISTORY

Janet Abu-Lughod's *Before European Hegemony*
Benedict Anderson's *Imagined Communities*
Bernard Bailyn's *The Ideological Origins of the American Revolution*
Hanna Batatu's *The Old Social Classes And The Revolutionary Movements Of Iraq*
Christopher Browning's *Ordinary Men: Reserve Police Batallion 101 and the Final Solution in Poland*
Edmund Burke's *Reflections on the Revolution in France*
William Cronon's *Nature's Metropolis: Chicago And The Great West*
Alfred W. Crosby's *The Columbian Exchange*
Hamid Dabashi's *Iran: A People Interrupted*
David Brion Davis's *The Problem of Slavery in the Age of Revolution*
Nathalie Zemon Davis's *The Return of Martin Guerre*
Jared Diamond's *Guns, Germs & Steel: the Fate of Human Societies*
Frank Dikotter's *Mao's Great Famine*
John W Dower's *War Without Mercy: Race And Power In The Pacific War*
W. E. B. Du Bois's *The Souls of Black Folk*
Richard J. Evans's *In Defence of History*
Lucien Febvre's *The Problem of Unbelief in the 16th Century*
Sheila Fitzpatrick's *Everyday Stalinism*

Eric Foner's *Reconstruction: America's Unfinished Revolution, 1863-1877*
Michel Foucault's *Discipline and Punish*
Michel Foucault's *History of Sexuality*
Francis Fukuyama's *The End of History and the Last Man*
John Lewis Gaddis's *We Now Know: Rethinking Cold War History*
Ernest Gellner's *Nations and Nationalism*
Eugene Genovese's *Roll, Jordan, Roll: The World the Slaves Made*
Carlo Ginzburg's *The Night Battles*
Daniel Goldhagen's *Hitler's Willing Executioners*
Jack Goldstone's *Revolution and Rebellion in the Early Modern World*
Antonio Gramsci's *The Prison Notebooks*
Alexander Hamilton, John Jay & James Madison's *The Federalist Papers*
Christopher Hill's *The World Turned Upside Down*
Carole Hillenbrand's *The Crusades: Islamic Perspectives*
Thomas Hobbes's *Leviathan*
Eric Hobsbawm's *The Age Of Revolution*
John A. Hobson's *Imperialism: A Study*
Albert Hourani's *History of the Arab Peoples*
Samuel P. Huntington's *The Clash of Civilizations and the Remaking of World Order*
C. L. R. James's *The Black Jacobins*
Tony Judt's *Postwar: A History of Europe Since 1945*
Ernst Kantorowicz's *The King's Two Bodies: A Study in Medieval Political Theology*
Paul Kennedy's *The Rise and Fall of the Great Powers*
Ian Kershaw's *The "Hitler Myth": Image and Reality in the Third Reich*
John Maynard Keynes's *The General Theory of Employment, Interest and Money*
Charles P. Kindleberger's *Manias, Panics and Crashes*
Martin Luther King Jr's *Why We Can't Wait*
Henry Kissinger's *World Order: Reflections on the Character of Nations and the Course of History*
Thomas Kuhn's *The Structure of Scientific Revolutions*
Georges Lefebvre's *The Coming of the French Revolution*
John Locke's *Two Treatises of Government*
Niccolò Machiavelli's *The Prince*
Thomas Robert Malthus's *An Essay on the Principle of Population*
Mahmood Mamdani's *Citizen and Subject: Contemporary Africa And The Legacy Of Late Colonialism*
Karl Marx's *Capital*
Stanley Milgram's *Obedience to Authority*
John Stuart Mill's *On Liberty*
Thomas Paine's *Common Sense*
Thomas Paine's *Rights of Man*
Geoffrey Parker's *Global Crisis: War, Climate Change and Catastrophe in the Seventeenth Century*
Jonathan Riley-Smith's *The First Crusade and the Idea of Crusading*
Jean-Jacques Rousseau's *The Social Contract*
Joan Wallach Scott's *Gender and the Politics of History*
Theda Skocpol's *States and Social Revolutions*
Adam Smith's *The Wealth of Nations*
Timothy Snyder's *Bloodlands: Europe Between Hitler and Stalin*
Sun Tzu's *The Art of War*
Keith Thomas's *Religion and the Decline of Magic*
Thucydides's *The History of the Peloponnesian War*
Frederick Jackson Turner's *The Significance of the Frontier in American History*
Odd Arne Westad's *The Global Cold War: Third World Interventions And The Making Of Our Times*

The Macat Library By Discipline

LITERATURE

Chinua Achebe's *An Image of Africa: Racism in Conrad's Heart of Darkness*
Roland Barthes's *Mythologies*
Homi K. Bhabha's *The Location of Culture*
Judith Butler's *Gender Trouble*
Simone De Beauvoir's *The Second Sex*
Ferdinand De Saussure's *Course in General Linguistics*
T. S. Eliot's *The Sacred Wood: Essays on Poetry and Criticism*
Zora Neale Huston's *Characteristics of Negro Expression*
Toni Morrison's *Playing in the Dark: Whiteness in the American Literary Imagination*
Edward Said's *Orientalism*
Gayatri Chakravorty Spivak's *Can the Subaltern Speak?*
Mary Wollstonecraft's *A Vindication of the Rights of Women*
Virginia Woolf's *A Room of One's Own*

PHILOSOPHY

Elizabeth Anscombe's *Modern Moral Philosophy*
Hannah Arendt's *The Human Condition*
Aristotle's *Metaphysics*
Aristotle's *Nicomachean Ethics*
Edmund Gettier's *Is Justified True Belief Knowledge?*
Georg Wilhelm Friedrich Hegel's *Phenomenology of Spirit*
David Hume's *Dialogues Concerning Natural Religion*
David Hume's *The Enquiry for Human Understanding*
Immanuel Kant's *Religion within the Boundaries of Mere Reason*
Immanuel Kant's *Critique of Pure Reason*
Søren Kierkegaard's *The Sickness Unto Death*
Søren Kierkegaard's *Fear and Trembling*
C. S. Lewis's *The Abolition of Man*
Alasdair MacIntyre's *After Virtue*
Marcus Aurelius's *Meditations*
Friedrich Nietzsche's *On the Genealogy of Morality*
Friedrich Nietzsche's *Beyond Good and Evil*
Plato's *Republic*
Plato's *Symposium*
Jean-Jacques Rousseau's *The Social Contract*
Gilbert Ryle's *The Concept of Mind*
Baruch Spinoza's *Ethics*
Sun Tzu's *The Art of War*
Ludwig Wittgenstein's *Philosophical Investigations*

POLITICS

Benedict Anderson's *Imagined Communities*
Aristotle's *Politics*
Bernard Bailyn's *The Ideological Origins of the American Revolution*
Edmund Burke's *Reflections on the Revolution in France*
John C. Calhoun's *A Disquisition on Government*
Ha-Joon Chang's *Kicking Away the Ladder*
Hamid Dabashi's *Iran: A People Interrupted*
Hamid Dabashi's *Theology of Discontent: The Ideological Foundation of the Islamic Revolution in Iran*
Robert Dahl's *Democracy and its Critics*
Robert Dahl's *Who Governs?*
David Brion Davis's *The Problem of Slavery in the Age of Revolution*

Alexis De Tocqueville's *Democracy in America*
James Ferguson's *The Anti-Politics Machine*
Frank Dikotter's *Mao's Great Famine*
Sheila Fitzpatrick's *Everyday Stalinism*
Eric Foner's *Reconstruction: America's Unfinished Revolution, 1863-1877*
Milton Friedman's *Capitalism and Freedom*
Francis Fukuyama's *The End of History and the Last Man*
John Lewis Gaddis's *We Now Know: Rethinking Cold War History*
Ernest Gellner's *Nations and Nationalism*
David Graeber's *Debt: the First 5000 Years*
Antonio Gramsci's *The Prison Notebooks*
Alexander Hamilton, John Jay & James Madison's *The Federalist Papers*
Friedrich Hayek's *The Road to Serfdom*
Christopher Hill's *The World Turned Upside Down*
Thomas Hobbes's *Leviathan*
John A. Hobson's *Imperialism: A Study*
Samuel P. Huntington's *The Clash of Civilizations and the Remaking of World Order*
Tony Judt's *Postwar: A History of Europe Since 1945*
David C. Kang's *China Rising: Peace, Power and Order in East Asia*
Paul Kennedy's *The Rise and Fall of Great Powers*
Robert Keohane's *After Hegemony*
Martin Luther King Jr.'s *Why We Can't Wait*
Henry Kissinger's *World Order: Reflections on the Character of Nations and the Course of History*
John Locke's *Two Treatises of Government*
Niccolò Machiavelli's *The Prince*
Thomas Robert Malthus's *An Essay on the Principle of Population*
Mahmood Mamdani's *Citizen and Subject: Contemporary Africa And The Legacy Of Late Colonialism*
Karl Marx's *Capital*
John Stuart Mill's *On Liberty*
John Stuart Mill's *Utilitarianism*
Hans Morgenthau's *Politics Among Nations*
Thomas Paine's *Common Sense*
Thomas Paine's *Rights of Man*
Thomas Piketty's *Capital in the Twenty-First Century*
Robert D. Putman's *Bowling Alone*
John Rawls's *Theory of Justice*
Jean-Jacques Rousseau's *The Social Contract*
Theda Skocpol's *States and Social Revolutions*
Adam Smith's *The Wealth of Nations*
Sun Tzu's *The Art of War*
Henry David Thoreau's *Civil Disobedience*
Thucydides's *The History of the Peloponnesian War*
Kenneth Waltz's *Theory of International Politics*
Max Weber's *Politics as a Vocation*
Odd Arne Westad's *The Global Cold War: Third World Interventions And The Making Of Our Times*

POSTCOLONIAL STUDIES

Roland Barthes's *Mythologies*
Frantz Fanon's *Black Skin, White Masks*
Homi K. Bhabha's *The Location of Culture*
Gustavo Gutiérrez's *A Theology of Liberation*
Edward Said's *Orientalism*
Gayatri Chakravorty Spivak's *Can the Subaltern Speak?*

PSYCHOLOGY

Gordon Allport's *The Nature of Prejudice*
Alan Baddeley & Graham Hitch's *Aggression: A Social Learning Analysis*
Albert Bandura's *Aggression: A Social Learning Analysis*
Leon Festinger's *A Theory of Cognitive Dissonance*
Sigmund Freud's *The Interpretation of Dreams*
Betty Friedan's *The Feminine Mystique*
Michael R. Gottfredson & Travis Hirschi's *A General Theory of Crime*
Eric Hoffer's *The True Believer: Thoughts on the Nature of Mass Movements*
William James's *Principles of Psychology*
Elizabeth Loftus's *Eyewitness Testimony*
A. H. Maslow's *A Theory of Human Motivation*
Stanley Milgram's *Obedience to Authority*
Steven Pinker's *The Better Angels of Our Nature*
Oliver Sacks's *The Man Who Mistook His Wife For a Hat*
Richard Thaler & Cass Sunstein's *Nudge: Improving Decisions About Health, Wealth and Happiness*
Amos Tversky's *Judgment under Uncertainty: Heuristics and Biases*
Philip Zimbardo's *The Lucifer Effect*

SCIENCE

Rachel Carson's *Silent Spring*
William Cronon's *Nature's Metropolis: Chicago And The Great West*
Alfred W. Crosby's *The Columbian Exchange*
Charles Darwin's *On the Origin of Species*
Richard Dawkin's *The Selfish Gene*
Thomas Kuhn's *The Structure of Scientific Revolutions*
Geoffrey Parker's *Global Crisis: War, Climate Change and Catastrophe in the Seventeenth Century*
Mathis Wackernagel & William Rees's *Our Ecological Footprint*

SOCIOLOGY

Michelle Alexander's *The New Jim Crow: Mass Incarceration in the Age of Colorblindness*
Gordon Allport's *The Nature of Prejudice*
Albert Bandura's *Aggression: A Social Learning Analysis*
Hanna Batatu's *The Old Social Classes And The Revolutionary Movements Of Iraq*
Ha-Joon Chang's *Kicking Away the Ladder*
W. E. B. Du Bois's *The Souls of Black Folk*
Émile Durkheim's *On Suicide*
Frantz Fanon's *Black Skin, White Masks*
Frantz Fanon's *The Wretched of the Earth*
Eric Foner's *Reconstruction: America's Unfinished Revolution, 1863-1877*
Eugene Genovese's *Roll, Jordan, Roll: The World the Slaves Made*
Jack Goldstone's *Revolution and Rebellion in the Early Modern World*
Antonio Gramsci's *The Prison Notebooks*
Richard Herrnstein & Charles A Murray's *The Bell Curve: Intelligence and Class Structure in American Life*
Eric Hoffer's *The True Believer: Thoughts on the Nature of Mass Movements*
Jane Jacobs's *The Death and Life of Great American Cities*
Robert Lucas's *Why Doesn't Capital Flow from Rich to Poor Countries?*
Jay Macleod's *Ain't No Makin' It: Aspirations and Attainment in a Low Income Neighborhood*
Elaine May's *Homeward Bound: American Families in the Cold War Era*
Douglas McGregor's *The Human Side of Enterprise*
C. Wright Mills's *The Sociological Imagination*

Thomas Piketty's *Capital in the Twenty-First Century*
Robert D. Putman's *Bowling Alone*
David Riesman's *The Lonely Crowd: A Study of the Changing American Character*
Edward Said's *Orientalism*
Joan Wallach Scott's *Gender and the Politics of History*
Theda Skocpol's *States and Social Revolutions*
Max Weber's *The Protestant Ethic and the Spirit of Capitalism*

THEOLOGY

Augustine's *Confessions*
Benedict's *Rule of St Benedict*
Gustavo Gutiérrez's *A Theology of Liberation*
Carole Hillenbrand's *The Crusades: Islamic Perspectives*
David Hume's *Dialogues Concerning Natural Religion*
Immanuel Kant's *Religion within the Boundaries of Mere Reason*
Ernst Kantorowicz's *The King's Two Bodies: A Study in Medieval Political Theology*
Søren Kierkegaard's *The Sickness Unto Death*
C. S. Lewis's *The Abolition of Man*
Saba Mahmood's *The Politics of Piety: The Islamic Revival and the Feminist Subject*
Baruch Spinoza's *Ethics*
Keith Thomas's *Religion and the Decline of Magic*

COMING SOON

Chris Argyris's *The Individual and the Organisation*
Seyla Benhabib's *The Rights of Others*
Walter Benjamin's *The Work Of Art in the Age of Mechanical Reproduction*
John Berger's *Ways of Seeing*
Pierre Bourdieu's *Outline of a Theory of Practice*
Mary Douglas's *Purity and Danger*
Roland Dworkin's *Taking Rights Seriously*
James G. March's *Exploration and Exploitation in Organisational Learning*
Ikujiro Nonaka's *A Dynamic Theory of Organizational Knowledge Creation*
Griselda Pollock's *Vision and Difference*
Amartya Sen's *Inequality Re-Examined*
Susan Sontag's *On Photography*
Yasser Tabbaa's *The Transformation of Islamic Art*
Ludwig von Mises's *Theory of Money and Credit*

Macat Disciplines

*Access the greatest ideas and thinkers
across entire disciplines, including*

AFRICANA STUDIES

Chinua Achebe's *An Image of Africa:
Racism in Conrad's Heart of Darkness*

W. E. B. Du Bois's *The Souls of Black Folk*

Zora Neale Hurston's *Characteristics of Negro Expression*

Martin Luther King Jr.'s *Why We Can't Wait*

Toni Morrison's *Playing in the Dark:
Whiteness in the American Literary Imagination*

Macat analyses are available from all good bookshops and libraries.

Access hundreds of analyses through one, multimedia tool.

Macat Disciplines

Access the greatest ideas and thinkers across entire disciplines, including

FEMINISM, GENDER AND QUEER STUDIES

Simone De Beauvoir's
The Second Sex

Michel Foucault's
History of Sexuality

Betty Friedan's
The Feminine Mystique

Saba Mahmood's
*The Politics of Piety:
The Islamic Revival and
the Feminist Subject*

Joan Wallach Scott's
*Gender and the
Politics of History*

Mary Wollstonecraft's
*A Vindication of the
Rights of Woman*

Virginia Woolf's
A Room of One's Own

Judith Butler's
Gender Trouble

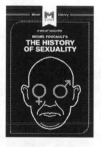

Macat analyses are available from all good bookshops and libraries.

Access hundreds of analyses through one, multimedia tool.
Join free for one month **library.macat.com**

Macat Disciplines

Access the greatest ideas and thinkers across entire disciplines, including

INEQUALITY

Ha-Joon Chang's, *Kicking Away the Ladder*

David Graeber's, *Debt: The First 5000 Years*

Robert E. Lucas's, *Why Doesn't Capital Flow from Rich To Poor Countries?*

Thomas Piketty's, *Capital in the Twenty-First Century*

Amartya Sen's, *Inequality Re-Examined*

Mahbub Ul Haq's, *Reflections on Human Development*

Macat analyses are available from all good bookshops and libraries.

Access hundreds of analyses through one, multimedia tool.

Join free for one month **library.macat.com**

Macat Disciplines

Access the greatest ideas and thinkers across entire disciplines, including

CRIMINOLOGY

Michelle Alexander's
The New Jim Crow: Mass Incarceration in the Age of Colorblindness

Michael R. Gottfredson & Travis Hirschi's
A General Theory of Crime

Elizabeth Loftus's
Eyewitness Testimony

Richard Herrnstein & Charles A. Murray's
The Bell Curve: Intelligence and Class Structure in American Life

Jay Macleod's
Ain't No Makin' It: Aspirations and Attainment in a Low-Income Neighborhood

Philip Zimbardo's
The Lucifer Effect

Printed in the United States
by Baker & Taylor Publisher Services